To El

from Paul

Nine Days' Wonder

FREDERICK GRICE

Nine Days' Wonder

Illustrated by Paul Ritchie

London
OXFORD UNIVERSITY PRESS
1976

Oxford University Press
OXFORD LONDON GLASGOW NEW YORK
TORONTO MELBOURNE WELLINGTON CAPE TOWN
IBADAN NAIROBI DAR ES SALAAM LUSAKA ADDIS ABABA
KUALA LUMPUR SINGAPORE JAKARTA HONG KONG TOKYO
DELHI BOMBAY CALCUTTA MADRAS KARACHI

ISBN 0 19 271394 9

First published 1976

To My Mother

Printed in Great Britain
by W & J Mackay Limited, Chatham

Contents

PART ONE
Grammar School Boy

PART TWO
The Nine Days

CONTENTS

PART THREE
Aftermath

PART ONE

Grammar School Boy

ONE

The First Day

The two boys who were starting the Grammar School together were not friends. They had been in the same class at the Junior School, and they were the only two boys from the school to win a scholarship, but they were not true friends. Chas Futer's father kept a draper's shop in the village, and lived in Windsor Gardens, and his mother didn't like him mixing with boys from the colliery. Keir's father worked at the Bishop Pit.

Chas was a heavy, fair-haired boy, with not much sense of fun. He was always called Chas because that was the name his mother gave him, and the name he always put on the outside of his exercise books. He was a timid, obstinate and possessive boy. He kept all his pens and rubbers in a wooden box with a sliding lid, and he hated lending anything.

Keir was just the opposite—a clumsy, impulsive, harum-scarum lad. He never seemed to know where the extremities of his body were. He tripped over carpets and kerbs and thresholds, and his knees were scarred with all the tosses he had taken. If he tried to knock in a nail he hit his finger. When he was sawing, the saw would jump out of the groove and rip his hand, and he was always bumping his head against something or other—a shelf, a corner of the mantelpiece, a lamp-post. He got his quickness and his clumsiness from his mother, who set about every little job she had to do as if she hadn't a minute to spare. When she threw a bucket of coal on the fire you would think she meant it to go straight through the wall. When she dried a plate she rubbed it so hard you would think she was trying to rub the pattern off. She constantly dropped things, cups and plates and saucers, and there was hardly a day when she did not appear with a rag tied around a finger she had cut when she had been sawing away at the loaf.

'There's a pair of you,' Keir's father would say. 'You're the clumsiest pair I've ivver seen in all my born days.' 'Well,' his mother would reply. 'I might be clumsy, but I'm not hot-headed like some folks I know. And if our Keir is always in trouble, it's easy to see where he gets that from. 'Cos you're a born trouble-maker. So he doesn't take after our side when it comes to getting into mischief.'

On their first day at the new school Chas and Keir kept together not because they liked each other's company, but because they were both in the same boat. Neither knew what to expect.

The approach to the school was by a narrow sloping street hemmed in on either side by tall tenements. High up in one of the houses a window had been pushed up, and two women were sitting on the window-sill, one of them with a baby. She was eating an apple, and as the boys went past she threw the core down and hit Chas on the shoulder. 'That nearly spoilt your new uniform, didn't it? I bet ye think a lot of yersels, gannen to the grammar school. Well, ye're nee better than anybody else!'

Chas walked on, but Keir picked up the core and made as if to throw it back, and the women drew back and slammed the window down. He threw the core into the air and kicked it. It left a wet stain on the toe of his boot.

The school puzzled Keir. There was a big entrance farther up the street, but he knew they hadn't to use that. He had used it when he had come for an interview a few months before, but one of the masters had caught him and told him it was for the staff only. The other entrance wasn't like the entrance to a school at all. You went down a dark passage, then down a flight of even darker steps, and came out into a long narrow playground. More steps led down to a shrubbery. Beyond the shrubbery was the river, and on the other side of the river, the castle and the cathedral.

No one told any of the new boys what to do. When the bell went they did what everybody else did, and went upstairs for 'Assem'. There were no chairs in the Assembly Hall. They all stood so tightly packed that there was hardly room to move. The new boys were all pushed to the front. Behind them were the second-formers, and the sixth-formers stood in a line along the side of the hall.

The Headmaster gave out the hymn

Lord, behold us with thy blessing,
Once again assembled here . . .

and the boys joined in with heavy, reluctant voices. Nearly all the masters were in gowns. One of them had thick black hair, and cheeks and jowl so blue you would think he had stained them with ink; and another, an older man, in a very high stiff collar and gold-rimmed spectacles, had his hands stuck vertically in his coat pockets with his thumbs outside. The Headmaster had a strange habit of making a funny, snorting noise before he spoke.

After Assembly the new boys were told to stay behind, and those who had done any French were given a test by a Jewish-looking teacher. After the test, Chas and Keir were told they had to go straight into the second form.

'That's lucky,' said Chas. 'We won't get ducked now.'

'What do you mean?'

'All the new boys have to get ducked, and then they have to go and see the ghost. But we'll be second-formers. They'll have to let us off.'

Keir wasn't frightened, but he couldn't help wondering what it was they did to new boys. What did they duck you in? In the river? Where was the ghost? After dinner he could see big boys prowling around the playground searching out the new boys and dragging them away. He had no idea where they were taking them, and wondered if they had got hold of Chas yet. The room that belonged to the form he had been put in was called Riverside. It stood all by itself, at the bottom of a flight of wooden steps. Nobody was allowed to go into the form-room during the dinner break, but he saw one or two other new boys trying to sneak down the steps.

He was hanging around at the top of the steps, waiting for the bell to go, when two big boys who looked like fourth or fifth-formers saw him.

'You're one of the new lads, aren't you?'

'Yes, but I'm in the second-form.'

'What do you mean?'

'I've gone straight into 2B.'

'What difference does that make? Have you been ducked?'

'No.'

'Get hold of him, Mick.'

They dragged him up the steps and across the playground into the toilets, where he could see the hand-basins ready filled with water. They pushed his head down into the icy water till he felt he could hold his breath no longer, but at the last moment they let go, pulled him out and marched him off, dripping, to a passage-way where a flight of worn steps mounted into a dark, unlit place. The cold water was running down the back of his neck, but he could not move his arms. Somebody had tied a scarf around his eyes. He was thrust forward and then something heavy and solid banged him on the top of his head.

'I am the ghost!' said a voice above him.

Keir hated being hurt. Whenever he was hit his instinct was to hit back. He wriggled free, pulled the scarf away from his eyes, and, looking up, saw a big grinning face, a big arm, and, at the end of the arm, a dustbin lid. He went for it but the bin lid caught him on the end of his nose. He was pulled away, and as he came out into the light, he saw that blood was pouring over his new school jacket and clean shirt front. He was trying to wash it off when the bell went for afternoon school.

'God in heaven,' said his mother when he got home. 'What have you been doing to your new school things?'

'Somebody made my nose bleed.'

'What a family I have! First it's your da and then it's you. Always fighting summat! Get that shirt off and see if I can get it clean. I dinna knaa what I've done to deserve a family like this.'

TWO

Two Years Later

That was two years ago. Now he was nearly fourteen and in the fourth-form. There was just one more term to go; then he would have to make up his mind whether he was going to take School Certificate or not.

On the first day Chas and he had travelled to school by train; but after a few weeks somebody in the County Offices had found out that they were within the three-mile limit, and the train passes were cancelled. Now they had to walk to school. He still walked with Chas, not because they were any better friends, but because they were still in the same form. Another boy had tagged on to them, a younger boy called Jimmy Metcalf. Keir had fallen into the habit of helping old Mr Metcalf to fill in his football coupons.

It was a long walk into the city and back again every day, and very heavy on boots and shoes. Keir's father had started to do his own cobbling and even tried soling his and Keir's shoes with rubber from old car tyres. Many of the miners' sons had their shoes soled with tyre rubber.

When he had first started school his father used to take him to Newcastle to see the Magpies playing. Once they went to see an international match between the English and the Scottish leagues; and one summer they had even gone on an excursion to Wembley to see the big Empire Exhibition. Keir had not slept much on the train, and fell asleep in one of the pavilions the next day. In those days his mother used to bring home a packet of whipped-cream walnuts every Saturday night; and sometimes when she did the shopping at Newcastle, while he and his father were at the match, they would come home with a carrier-bag filled with fruit.

But the weekly pay packet was smaller now, and hardly a week went past without the caller coming round to tell the men that the pit was going to close down for a day or maybe two days. When the gramophone they had bought just after the war broke down they could not afford to get it mended. In the end they gave everything except the horn to the rag-and-bone man.

But at school little had changed except that old Johnny Pollock had left. As they walked to school that morning, the first morning of the last term of the year, Keir wondered who their new form-master would be. Their old form-master had been Johnny Pollock.

Johnny Pollock had been the worst teacher in the school. He couldn't control the boys and they were always playing jokes on him. As soon as he came into the classroom the boy in one corner of the room would bang his desk lid down, or give a loud cough or a sneeze, the one behind him would follow suit, and the bang or the cough or the sneeze would go right round the class while old Johnny stood looking on, feeble and helpless. On the few occasions when he tried to cuff a boy, the boy in the next desk would give a frightful sneeze, and say, 'Nearly gave me pneumonia, sir! The draught from that swipe!'

Johnny taught French and he used to give out copies of *La France*. There were only five or six copies so the boys had to sit in groups. Keir discovered that there was a joke corner in the paper—corny old jokes that nobody in his right senses would be amused by:

Pourquoi Napoleon resemble-t-il à un miroir?
Parce qu'il est bien poli.

Keir got all his group to burst out in a wild guffaw, and when old Johnny came over to see what the matter was, he would point to the item in the magazine and say, 'Joke, sir! A French joke! It makes you laugh, sir!' and then they would all burst out again in noisy howls and guffaws. Johnny never knew how to react. He could never make up his mind whether the boys were pulling his leg or really enjoying the joke. And while he was dithering another group behind him would break out into the same raucous din. 'Moderate your mirth, boys,' he would say feebly. 'Moderate your mirth.' And he sounded so funny that the whole class started to laugh at him.

Assembly began once more. The sixth-formers were all lined up as usual down the side of the crowded hall. The Head marched past them like a general reviewing his troops. All the masters were in gowns except the Art Master and the Woodwork Master. Old Johnny wasn't there. In his place there was a gaunt man, tall, black-faced, with a long scraggy neck and big ears, and his mouth shut tight as if he had something between his teeth and didn't want to let go of it. When they sang the familiar hymn

Lord, behold us . . .

he didn't sing, but kept his mouth tight shut.

As Keir feared, the new teacher had taken Johnny's place, as their new form-master. He swept into the form-room and said, 'Stand, everybody!'

They stood noisily.

'Right, sit! Now that's the last time I'll give you that command—get it? As soon as I come in, you stand—until I tell you to sit down. All right—get it? Now sit up straight. What's the matter with you, boy, been up all night or something? No slouching, and give me your names in alphabetical order. Surname first. Then Christian names—names, note, not just name. The names you were baptised with, not the names your doting parents give you. A's first. Hands up the A's.'

'Addison, sir, Norman.'

'Right.'

'Anthony, sir.'

'Not your Christian name, stupid. Surname.'

'That is my surname, sir. Anthony, John David.'

'Beg your pardon, Anthony John David. Any more A's?'

Keir hated this business of calling out names. If he had been called William or Henry or George he wouldn't have minded. Why had his father given him so stupid a name? He waited irritably for the fatuous comment that always came when he gave his name.

'Ramsay, sir, Keir.'

'Keir Ramsay?'

'Yes, sir.'

'Not very difficult to see which side of the fence your father is on, is it? A double dose of the red, eh? With a name like that you'll be a very welcome guest at the Kremlin, won't you? Next.'

He collected all the names, but he did not tell them his name. When he had finished the register he looked up at Keir, and said, 'You—yes, you—with the agitator's name—clean that blackboard, and see that it's clean whenever I come into this room. Got that? Good.'

'What's his name, Chas?' shouted Keir, as soon as the master had gone. Chas was the one who always knew what it was correct to know.

'Whose name?' he replied pettishly.

'This new form-master, you fathead. Who else?'

'He's Mr Smelley.'

'What?'

'But you don't spell it that way. You have to spell it with an 'ey' at the end. S-m-e-l-l-e-y.'

'Hey,' shouted Keir. 'It's Smelley! It's Smelley!' And, pinching his nostrils with his fingers, he screwed up his face. 'Stinker Smelley!'

It was the obvious nickname, and from then on Mr Smelley was Stinker to every boy in the school, except perhaps Chas.

In the middle of the afternoon Major Goldie came in to take them for History. Keir hated this lesson. Major Goldie never did anything but dictate notes to them—the causes of the War of the Spanish Succession, the events of the War of the Spanish Succession, the results of the War of the Spanish Succession. This time the lesson was on the Abolition of Slavery and he began his dreary dictation—slavery before the birth of Wilberforce; incidents in the life of William Wilberforce; results of the Abolition of Slavery in America. . . . No sooner had the lesson started than the afternoon bell began to ring from the cathedral—ding-dong, ding-dong, ding-dong—a monotonous seesaw of sound that seemed to be imitating the boring voice of Major Goldie reciting his dry notes. Keir sat yawning and copying the dry facts into his jotter, waiting for the dull sing-song of the cathedral bell to end. It always stopped at five to three, tolled for five minutes and then struck the hour and fell silent. As soon as it struck the hour he knew that the lesson was nearly at an end.

He gave a huge yawn, and at that moment Major Goldie looked up and caught him.

'What's the matter with you, Ramsay? You find this boring, do you? I should have thought with a name like yours you would have been thrilled with this particular piece of history. Copy out the Results of the Abolition of Slavery—all of them, all five of them—ten times for me tonight. . . . And that may remind you not to yawn in my lessons.'

Keir was writing out his imposition when his father came in.

'That homework is tekkin' a bit of finishing, isn't it?'

'It's an imposition. I have to write it out ten times for yawning in class. It's about the Abolition of Slavery.'

'Which one give you that?'

'The History Master, Major Goldie.'

'What, him?'

'Do you know him?'

'Is there anybody that dissent? He's a flaming double-dyed Tory if ivver there was one. The abolition of slavery, by God! Slavery will nivver be abolished in this country as lang as there are fellers like him.'

'What's the matter with him?'

'He's the one that's trying to get hissel put forward as a Tory candidate for this division. He'll get mair than he bargains for if he comes looking for votes in this constituency. Abolition of slavery—chuck it in the fire!'

'I daren't do that, da. He's a teacher.'

'Major Goldie! I wonder what right he has to call hissel a major. I'll give him a bit of my mind if ivver I see him. Aye, for two pins, I'd write to him this minute.'

'Don't do that, da. Don't say anything to him. It's bad enough as it is.'

'What's bad enough?'

'They all pull my leg as it is.'

'Who does?'

'The teachers.'

'What about?'

'About my name.'

'Do they, by God? Well, just tell them if they had as good a name as you've got they'd be a sight better off. Ye get your name from one of the best friends the working man ivver had. Keir Hardie—that was the man. And if we had a few more

Keir Hardies now we wadden't be where we are. Flaming Tories!'

'Oh for heaven's sake, Davy, let it drop. The poor bairn has enough to contend with,' said Keir's mother, 'without setting him against his teachers. Let it drop. We've had enough politics for one day. Let's have a bit of peace afore we get to bed. It's politics politics from morn to night in this house. Let him finish off his homework and get to bed at a decent time for once.'

Her husband said no more, but Keir could see that something had vexed him. Maybe the pit was going to close down again. He turned back to his imposition and went on scribbling.

Often when he was sitting in his corner copying out some boring impot or trying to work out a problem that baffled him he would hear his father and his friends talking politics, going over some announcement by the government, or some defiant call by the men's leaders.

His father was always talking about politics these days—about the Sankey Award and the Nationalisation of the mines, about men like Herbert Smith and A. J. Cook. 'Aye, A. J. Cook's the lad to lead us,' he would say. 'He's the feller with the right ideas.

Not a minute on the day,
Not a penny off the pay!

That should be painted on ivvery banner in the country.'

But Keir didn't understand what his father was so concerned about. It was more than he could do to keep up with all those other vexatious problems he was expected to master—quadratic equations, the principles of magnetism, the War of the Spanish Succession and daft poems like that one called Ode on the Pleasures arising from Vicissitude. That was the most stupid one of the lot. What that long word 'vicissitude' meant he hadn't the faintest idea.

THREE

The Colliery and the Village

One of the things Keir had to do for homework was to learn the causes of the War of Jenkins' Ear. He put off doing it though he knew that Major Goldie would test them and pick on him to repeat the list for him; and when at last he sat down to it he found that he had left his Warner and Martin in his desk. There was only one thing to do—go and ask Chas if he could look at his. Chas never forgot his books. He was too much of a goody-goody for that.

He walked down Brunel Street, and through the gap between Brunel and Stephenson Street he saw the skips going up and down the overhead cable that led from the pithead to the top of the big slagheap, climbing slowly, pausing when they came to the top, tipping and shooting down the dusty rubble in a black smudge, then swinging loosely as they came back to bank. The pulley wheels were spinning fast, and every now and then he could hear the sound of the cage clanging as it came to rest at the top of the shaft, and the rapping of the onsetter as he signalled to the winding-engine man.

Then he walked across the bridge, and as the road opened in front of him he saw the village square with its little white-washed town-hall at the far end.

The village had been there long before the great Bishop Pit

had been sunk, and the green, which was no longer a green but a big wedge-shaped asphalted space, was surrounded by old houses. There was one with a sun-dial on the wall, but the pointer was rusted and nobody could make out the inscription above it. In front of the town hall was a small triangular garden with two memorials, one to the men who died in the 1914–1918 war, and another to an overman who had given his life trying to save two boys trapped in the Bishop Pit. A few old men were sitting on the seats smoking and spitting.

In the little kiosk in the entrance to the Empire Cinema a woman was sitting counting the takings for the night, and as the door of the Nicky Nack opened a smell of beer and tobacco poured out of it. Keir hurried past, crossed the square and made for the street where Chas lived.

Chas's father, Mr Futers, kept the Hassop Outfitting Emporium in a shop on the square. He was a stickler for ready money, and didn't like giving credit, but he was a clever business man, and you could pick up a bargain there. He lived where most of the better-off lived, in a row of villas called Windsor Gardens. That was its proper name, but it was better known as Poverty Street, because most of the people who lived there had a reputation for being stingy. The tramps and beggars had a thin time there. They did much better in the colliery streets on the other side of the bridge.

Keir knocked on the door of Number Five. You couldn't just walk into the house as you could in the colliery. You had to knock and wait. Mr Futers came to the door with a green shade over his eyes and a pen in his hand. He didn't ask Keir in. He just asked what he wanted and left him on the doorstep. When Chas came to the door he said he couldn't lend Keir the book but if he liked he could come in and copy down the bit that he wanted.

Keir hated going into Number Five. It always seemed cold and unwelcoming; and he didn't like the way in which Mr

Futers always looked at his boots to see if they were clean; and he didn't like his sarcastic manner.

'Forgotten your book again, eh? You'd forget your head if it was loose. You're a feckless lot, aren't you? Well, sit down and do what you have to do. And don't take too long over it.'

Keir said nothing but began to copy out the work he had to do on the piece of paper he had brought with him. Mr Futers sounded as if he didn't want to be interrupted, but he didn't mind interrupting Keir.

'Yes, you have to have your head screwed on the right way if you want to run a business nowadays. I haven't the time to sit boozing and gambling like some I know. It's a good thing for you to have our Chas to fall back upon, isn't it?'

Keir was glad to get away from the house into the noisy, comfortable, colliery streets. That stuck-up shopkeeper! Keir couldn't bear him, with his nasty sneering ways and his cold cheerless house. When he came to Brunel Street he found Pompey Allchurch and another lad kicking a ball about. He joined them, and when a wild kick sent the ball rattling against one of the street windows, an old woman rushed out and began to shout at them.

'Mind if ye brik one of my winders with that ball you'll have to pay for it! Get yersels away and play at the other end of the street!'

'What's the matter, Bella?' asked her neighbour, who had also come to the door.

'It's that cheeky Pompey Allchurch—and young Keir Ramsay's nee better either. They're always into mischief, them two. They'll have the pollis after them one of these days.'

They moved off, but the boy whose ball it was had to go in. Keir mouched around with Pompey, throwing stones at the pot insulators on the top of the telegraph poles to see if they could crack them, until it began to get dark. When Keir got back home he found his mother in a bad temper. She ordered him off to bed. He took his homework with him, but as soon as he had smoothed out the paper on which he had copied out the causes of the War of Jenkins' Ear, the electric bulb in his room began to flicker and went out. He shouted down to tell his mother that the bulb had gone.

'I've got a spare one somewhere,' she called back to him. 'Aye, here it is. I'll just rub it wi' the duster.'

He heard the cupboard go bang, and then something falling with a crash on to the floor.

'What's happened?'

'The thing just slipped reet out of my fingers, Keir. You'd think it was wick.'

'Have you got another one?'

'No, that's the last.'

'What about my homework?'

'You'll just have to leave it till the morning. Mind I dinna think much of these bulbs. They're just like a bit of soap in your hands.'

Keir tried to make out the words of his notes by the faint light that came in through the window. But it was too dark to see them properly. Jenkins' Ear would have to wait. He would get Chas to test him on the long walk to school. And if Chas wouldn't help him little Jimmy Metcalf would. Jimmy was an infernal nuisance tagging on, but he was a good-natured little lad and he would do anything for Keir.

FOUR

The Cundy

The old part of the slagheap, the part that had been made before they installed the overhead railway, was like one of the battlefields that Keir had seen pictures of in his History of the Great War, pock-marked with craters like shell-holes. A few weeds grew there, coltsfoot, which the men would dry and smoke when they couldn't afford baccy, and a flower like a dog-daisy that gave off a queer smell when you trod on it. But the newer part of the tip was black and stony and ended in a steep scree down which the spoil from the pit was tipped from the overhead cable line that led to the top. The loose spoil spilled over the field below it, spreading like lava and engulfing grass, shrubs and trees. At its lower edges it had flowed around a few stunted oaks and alders, leaving them half-buried like men in a quicksand. The bare leafless branches rose above the rubble like the hands and arms of drowning men; and beyond them, as yet unreached by the black tide, shivered other doomed trees, their foliage already shrivelling in the fumes blown from the tip.

It was under this mountain of rubble that the Cundy lay—a long culvert built to let the waters of a small stream drain through. No one could remember when it had been built, and nobody that Keir knew had ever got through it. A few yards beyond the entrance some one had put up a grating to keep boys and animals out.

For Pompey Allchurch forbidden territory like the Cundy was an irresistible temptation, for he was the master mischief-maker of the colliery boys, and the bane of every law-abiding woman in Hassop. He smashed the pots on the tops of telegraph poles by throwing stones at them, tried to ride the pit ponies that had been brought to bank, tormented old women by stuffing paper up their rain-water pipes and setting fire to it, kicked balls through windows, raided allotments and played Knocky-Nine-Door up and down the dark streets, rapping on doors and banging gates. He was one of the boys whom Keir had left behind when he went to the Grammar School, but he still liked to play with him. He always had something interesting in his pockets, something he had picked up or snaffled. He always had something to show—or to do.

It was Pompey who first had the idea of getting into the Cundy. He had found a hacksaw on the tip, and laid his hands somehow on an old carbide lamp.

'I know how to use a hacksaw and I've lit the lamp once,' he said. 'It's great!' Both his statements were lies, but lies came naturally to Pompey.

As soon as they got into the Cundy he tried to light the lamp. When he poured the water on to the carbide it began to sizzle and fizz. It wouldn't light, but he pricked the nozzle with a pin, and they began to smell the gas coming through. It caught fire and began to burn with a dazzlingly brilliant flame that hurt Keir's eyes, but he held it away from him and Pompey set to work with the hacksaw. The bars of the grating were rusty and tough but before the lamp went out they managed to get one loose. There was still not enough room to get through but they filled the lamp again and freed another bar. Now there was room enough for them to squeeze through, but before they could get very far the lamp spluttered and went out. Pompey had no more carbide, but they didn't mind much. The first job had been done successfully. They would have to come back another day, but at least they had done what nobody else had done—they had found a way into the Cundy.

A week later, when Pompey had got hold of more carbide and cleaned up his lamp, they went back. Nobody had touched the two bars they had loosened. They removed them, lit the lamp and began their exploration. The bottom of the tunnel was wet and muddy, and once or twice Keir felt the water coming over the tops of his boots. He tried to keep to the side, but he could feel his coat brushing against the damp brick-work of the tunnel. Then the passage seemed to take a turn and they could no longer see behind them the oval mouth of the Cundy.

From time to time they heard the plopping of water as it dripped from the roof of the tunnel, and there were mysterious scufflings and splashings ahead of them as if some creatures—were they rats?—were retreating before them. There was nothing exciting to be found, nothing more than a few rusty tins and lengths of wet wood that had been swept down by the stream, and pale plants sprouting from the furred and glistening brickwork. But suddenly they saw a grey form run away from them and then turn, its wicked red eyes flashing in the light of the lamp before it turned again and vanished. Then in the far darkness there were visible more sharp pinpricks of light glittering back at them as if a legion of rats was waiting in the shadows for them. They turned and retreated.

Some time later Pompey said to Keir, 'Eh, Keir, I got one of them rats in the Cundy.'

'Killed it?'

'Yeh. Billy Sumner let me use his airgun. And I got one first shot.'

'What have you done with it?'

'I've got it. In this bag. I'm gonna leave it on Mrs Pratt's step.'

'What for?'

'She's always telling us off about playing in the street and always complaining to our dad about me. I'm gonna pay her back. She'll jump when she sees this on her step, I bet.'

It was getting dark and nobody saw them dump the rat on Mrs Pratt's doorstep, but just as Pompey was turning it over on to its stomach and making it look as if it was crawling across the step, the door of the next house opened, and a man's voice said, 'What are you two up to, eh?'

They didn't stop to answer but ran, and behind them they could hear the voice: 'Ye needn' run away. I knaa who ye are, ye wicked little nowts!'

That night Keir was again in disgrace.

'Sometimes I think you haven't the sense you were born with,' his mother said. 'Ye might have given that poor old woman heart failure! Did ye nivver think of that? Honestly, it beats me what young lads are coming to these days. Mind if you try any mair of them tricks, I'll bray the wick out of ye. You'd better get off to bed afore your da comes in, because if he gets to know what ye've been up to he'll give you summat you'll not forget in a hurry."

'But, ma, I have to do my homework.'

'Ye should ha thought of that when you were runnin' around with that Pompey Allchurch. Get off to bed, and not another word.'

FIVE

The Crystal Set

The Alderman Watson Grammar School was made up of an assortment of buildings strung out along the riverside. The main building was a high red-brick structure of several storeys, labs and classrooms at the bottom and the hall at the top. The hall was so small that the boys had to stand for 'Assem'; but the Art Room was large and lofty, with big arched windows like the windows of a church, set so high that you could see nothing out of them but the sky. Every now and then Mr Frogmore, the old teacher whom Keir had noticed with his hands stuck in his pockets on his first day at school, would startle the class by calling out, 'Pencils down everyone! Look out of the window!' as if he wanted to draw their attention to some aeroplane or airship or wonderful bird; but all he wanted to do was to get them to look at the clouds.

'Look at the clouds! Keep looking! You'll never see clouds like those wherever you go—France, Italy, Spain. Beautiful clouds! Beautiful clouds!'

Most of the boys thought he was dotty, but they respected him because he was a good artist, and when the weather was fine he would take them into Wharton Park to sketch. There was a rumour that he had some pictures hanging on the walls in the Art Gallery at Newcastle.

The far end of the Art Room was filled with plaster casts of nudes—Greek gods and goddesses—incongruous figures that nobody ever made the slightest use of, except to make rude jokes about them. Keir's mother had been very shocked by them when she came to attend his one and only medical (the medicals were held in the Art Room). She was so startled by them that she could hardly listen to what the doctor had to say. Fortunately Keir was as strong as a pit pony and there was nothing wrong except that his teeth wanted filling. When he got home that night, she said, in a pained voice, 'Mind, it's a queer place that school of yours. I don't think you should have things like what you have in that classroom. They're not decent.' And later he heard her saying to Mrs Pratt, one of her neighbours, 'Ee, Hannah, there wasn't a stitch on any one of them, as true as I'm standing here. Ye've nivver seen nowt like it. I didn't knaa where to look.'

The third and fourth-forms had their form-rooms in what was called the North School, a warren of old rooms that had once been parts of dwelling houses. There were radiators in the newer part of the school where the Art Room was, but the North School was heated by old-fashioned cylindrical stoves. The boys liked these stoves. In the cold weather they crowded round them and dropped things into them.

It was a small school and most of the subjects had only one teacher. Nearly all the History lessons were taken by Major Goldie. He was a lazy teacher, scornful and sarcastic, and his lessons were boring, for he did little more than dictate notes, rubbing away at his blue jowl as if he was trying to rub the dark stain even more deeply into his chin. While he droned away Keir would listen to the cathedral bell going ding-dong, ding-dong, ding-dong for twenty minutes before it came to three o'clock, as if it, too, was weary of the endless dictation and the endless scribbling of the boys as they copied Major Goldie's dry-as-dust notes into their books.

But Mr Howard, the Latin master, was a different story. The young boys in the first form had a jingle

Latin is a dead tongue,
Dead as dead can be.
First it killed the Romans,
Now it's killing me.

But it wasn't a dead tongue to Micky Howard. The door of the dingy classroom would fly open and in he blew, the tails of his old gown flying out behind him. He went straight to his desk, took out his pencil and began to roll it vigorously up and down between his palms. He always did this, making the pencil click against the gold ring on his left hand. His thinning hair was plastered flat over the top of his head, and his sharp nose and cheeks shone. He always walked to school, and he kept the fresh colour in his cheeks long after Assembly.

'Right,' he would say. 'The world's upside down but the Latin language lives for ever. The verb—amo amare—present tense. Amo, amas, amat . . .'

They all joined in. Mr Howard had gone through the war without a scratch, and now he meant to get his class through all the declensions and conjugations of the Latin tongue with no casualties. He drove them on, doubled them back, manœuvred them up and down, and when they came to the end of their drill they felt braced and ready for anything.

The best thing about him was that you never knew what he was going to do next—except on Armistice Day. Every November 11, after the two minutes' silence, he would say, 'Put your books away! Never forget that terrible war! Never! Sit up straight in your desks and I'll tell you about it.'

Then they would all forget that they were in a class-room listening to a teacher, and he would tell them stories of strafes and bombardments, of waiting for zero hour in the sodden trenches, of going over the top and plunging into the smoke and mud of No Man's Land, hearing the cries of the wounded and the call for stretcher-bearers. Some of the boys said he had been a captain in the Durham Light Infantry, but he never called himself captain. Goldie was the one who paraded his title.

Sometimes he would bring in his gramophone and a few records.

'You've had enough of Latin for one week,' he would say. 'Let's have some refreshment for the spirit, shall we? Listen to this.'

And he would play some classical music, taking advantage of the end of the record to explain how carefully and cleverly the music was arranged, and how the melody was transferred from one instrument to another.

He was the one teacher that Keir wanted to work for. He didn't know how it was but in the presence of this man he seemed to become quicker and cleverer. Once they had a passage to translate that none of them had ever seen before. Mr Howard wouldn't tell them any of the difficult words till they had done their best to work them out for themselves. At one point they came to the word 'magus'. Nobody knew it. They hadn't seen it before.

'Work it out,' he said. 'You can do it. Get the plural and think where you've seen it before. What about the Scriptures? What about the Gospel? There now, I've given you a clue.'

Suddenly Keir saw it.

'It means "a wise man".'

'Right. Right. That's good. Now you're really using your brains!'

This was what happened over and over again between Keir and Mr Howard. Something jumped from one to the other like a spark between two terminals. There was a flash and the answer jumped into Keir's mind.

But it happened with nobody else, and certainly not with Major Goldie, or with Mr Smelley, the new form master. Fortunately he didn't take them for anything. But they knew that he would take them for Maths when they got into the fifth.

School Certificate was still a year away, so the Fourth-form still took Woodwork. They had a double period for Woodwork every Friday morning before Games. The games field was a long way away from the school, and it took twenty minutes to walk there. To save time they changed into their football strip immediately after prayers and then went to Woodwork. Mr Gladwell used to walk round the room with a steel rule in his hand, slapping the backsides of the boys who were doing anything wrong. It wasn't too bad if you had ordinary trousers on, but with thin football shorts it used to sting. Mr Gladwell could be very cutting and sarcastic when he liked. Once he was demonstrating something to the class and asked Keir to bring him a set-square. Keir brought him a T-Square instead and Mr Gladwell held it up and said, 'What do you think? Here's a chap that's been doing Woodwork for more than two years, and he doesn't know the difference between a set-square and a T-square. Pull yourself together, Ramsay, pull yourself together.'

Everybody laughed. They knew that Mr Gladwell wanted them to laugh. Keir didn't like being laughed at and made a fool of. Nor did he like the silly things they had to spend their time making, like pipe racks. He didn't know anybody who used a pipe rack.

Sometimes Mr Gladwell would come late. He would be missing from 'Assem'. Then when they went into the Woodwork Room he would give everybody something to get on with, and ask Chas to keep an eye on the door while he gave himself a shave. He used to shave in a big sheet of tin propped up on a bench.

But Keir didn't dislike him too much, because he took the class for Maths as well and Keir was good at Maths when he tried. Although Mr Gladwell had shown him up in Woodwork once, he praised him for his Algebra, and said his was the best Algebra homework book he'd ever seen. But the best thing he ever did for Keir was to help him make a crystal set.

He would not let any of the boys start on their sets till they gave him a promise that they would buy all the parts they couldn't make—the condenser, the crystal, the cat's whisker and the earphones.

Keir's father looked troubled when he asked if he could make his crystal set.

'We're a bit pushed for the time being. How much will it cost?'

'It might be more than a pound.'

'Might be better not to think about it, yet, bonny lad. We've been laid off a bit lately. I waddent like to see mysel out o' work and with debts on my back.'

Fortunately Keir did not have to trouble his father about the money. He made threepence here and there shovelling into the coalhouses the coals that were tipped on the pavement by the colliery carts. He went errands for his aunts, and he won three-and-sixpence in a drawing competition run by Brooke Bond Tea. And Mr Metcalf always made a point of giving him something out of his winnings.

Mr Metcalf, Jimmy's father, was a quiet smiling little man whose great passion was filling in football coupons. Every Thursday night he would clear the table and set out his coupons in front of him and try to forecast five homes, or three draws or four aways. But he didn't like to begin till Keir came.

'Here's my little seggertary,' he would say. 'This is the lad that brings me luck.'

Mr Metcalf could not hold a pen properly—he had arthritis in his right hand—and his own son Jimmy was too impatient with him, and too fond of kicking a ball about in the yard or in the street to be of much use to him. But Keir liked helping him, looking through the league tables and sizing up the form of the teams. There was something about the names of the teams that fascinated him—Aston Villa, Tottenham Hotspur, Queen of the South, Hamilton Academicals, Crystal Palace; and he could have drawn a wonderful map of England and Scotland labelled not with the names of capes and rivers but with the great football grounds—Highbury, St James's Park, Stamford Bridge, the Hawthorns, Deepdale, Ibrox etc.

And they were lucky. They didn't always lose; and when Mr Metcalf's three draws or five homes came up he always gave a share of his winnings to Keir.

'There tha' is, lad. Tek it and keep it. The labourer is worthy of his hire.'

So with one thing and another Keir saved the money he wanted, and Mr Gladwell let him start on the set. While Keir was working on the coil, patiently wrapping the fine copper wire around the cylinder and fixing the tuning knob, he told him what kind of things he might hear. 'With a bit of luck you might get 2 LO—that's London. It's a long way from here but the signal's strong. In any case you're bound to get 5 NO because that's Newcastle, and Newcastle's on the doorstep. Keep working the cat's whisker till you get a good spot on the crystal. And if you do find a good spot stick to it.'

In the end Keir finished it to Mr Gladwell's satisfaction. He couldn't try it out in school because there was no aerial but Mr Gladwell was certain it would work. His mother wouldn't let him fix up an aerial in the kitchen. She was making a mat and the big wooden frames filled the room, and almost every night some neighbour or other dropped in to give a hand with the work. At last, however, seeing how disappointed Keir was, she said he could fix the aerial up in the Room.

It was really the sitting-room, but it was always called the

Room, as if it was the only part of the house that was entitled to that name. There was a big square table in the middle of the room, its varnished surface covered with a dark green plush cloth, its legs wrapped in old stockings to keep them from being kicked or scratched. Against the wall opposite the fireplace there was a big press, the bottom half made up of drawers and the top half of a cupboard which was usually kept locked, because it contained the best china and all the family papers—birth certificates, marriage lines, insurance policies and checks from the co-op. By the window there was a plant stand with an aspidistra, and in the corner a whatnot. The lower shelves were filled with little jugs and trinkets with the coat of arms of Saltburn, Roker, Blackpool and other places the family had once visited; and on the upper shelves photographs of relatives; his aunt Linda sitting at a marble-topped table in front of a picture of Durham Cathedral, his uncles in uniform, and embroidered cards sent from Lille, Arras, Armentières. But pride-of-place went to his father's favourites, two big photographs in silver frames, one of a hairy, bearded old man with 'Keir Hardie, Founder of the I.L.P.' stamped in gilt letters under his beard; and the other a younger, more handsome man 'Ramsay Macdonald, our First Prime Minister'.

When he had first become aware of these strange faces, Keir had asked his father if they too were relatives.

'I wish they were,' his father had said. 'I'd be a proud man if I was related to them.'

'Who are they then?'

'The best friends the working man has ivver had.'

'Am I called after them?'

'After that one,' said Mr Ramsay, pointing to the bearded man.

'Why?'

'I picked that name for tha. And tha'll be proud of it afore tha's finished.'

But Keir didn't think so, and he could never look at the faces of those two strangers on the whatnot without feeling that it was all their fault that he had such a daft name. Why couldn't he have been given an ordinary name like Fred or Tommy or Harry? Sometimes when he went into the Room he would see those two serious faces staring at him as if they were saying, 'We're the ones that gave you your names and you'd better live up to them.' Then he would turn their faces to the wall so that he could not see them glaring at him, and looking as if they meant to decide his life for him just as they had forced their names upon him.

Keir hated his namesakes, but the Room was a good room for listening in. The fire was not lit from one month's end to another, and the place was as cold as Christmas, but nobody kept coming and going. He had it to himself.

He strung up his aerial, a long trail of wire that went along the picture rail and behind the whatnot, sat down with the earphones clamped on his head and began to move the tuning knob backwards and forwards. At first he could hear nothing at all, but after he had fiddled with the knob and the crystal, he began to get his first sounds, a vague shushing noise that transformed itself into music. It was very cold in the unheated room, and with every minute his fingers grew colder and colder, but at last by some lucky stroke the cat's whisker lighted on a good spot, and the sounds of a jazz band came loud and clear and marvellously sweet. The Savoy Orpheans! It was his first message from the air. He ran into the kitchen and asked his mother to come and listen, but she knocked the set when she was sitting down and the cat's whisker moved.

But Keir knew now that his wireless set worked, and from then on he spent many an hour that ought to have been given to his homework listening to anything that came on the air—jazz, brass bands, Count John MacCormack, and, once, the sound of a nightingale from the Surrey woods.

SIX

Trespassing

It was mid-April. The brittle alders by the allotments had put out their dusty leaves. There were coltsfoot flowers growing out of the cinders between the rails, and in the open countryside the hedges were greening over. The sports and games of the winter evenings—Bump-the-Cuddy, Knocky-Nine Door, Tally-ho—were forgotten, and Keir and Pompey spent most of their spare time birds'-nesting, not only in the common fields and along the common hedges, but in the woods and copses of Bendlestone Hall, the big estate that lay near to Hassop. It was forbidden territory, guarded by the dreaded figure of the gamekeeper; but everything that was taboo was fair game for Pompey and Keir. They climbed over the stone wall that enclosed the park, scratched their wrists as they thrust their hands deeper and deeper into the hawthorns, greened over their clothes and hands by climbing in hollies, and scaled higher trees to reach the flat, twiggy nests of wood-pigeons—always on the look-out for the enemy of enemies, the gamekeeper, who was ready to raise his gun and bring them down like a rook or a rabbit; to seize them and force their names from them and pass them on to the policeman, who would come crossing the yard at home with the dreaded summons in his hand.

One day Pompey told Keir he had found a pheasant's nest in the wood. It had two eggs when he found it, but he thought that by now it might have five or six. 'That's three apiece. And you can eat pheasant's eggs, ye know. They're good for you.'

Pompey was always hungry. He would eat anything—turnips from the fields, blackberries and bilberries, little white roots called 'arnicks' that he dug up, even 'cheese and bread', the fresh green hawthorn shoots, and haws. He loved sucking birds' eggs.

That day a deep silence seemed to hang over the wood. The clattering of a wood pigeon breaking cover startled Keir like an alarm, and the snapping of twigs beneath his feet sounded like a signal for an outburst of firing from hidden marksmen. He always felt like this in a wood, with the brambles clutching at his stockings and pulling them down to his ankles, and the peppery smell of the dead leaves stinging his nostrils. He always felt the same—a tingling sense of danger, of being in the presence of mysterious creatures that slipped away and eluded him as he advanced. The wood stretched ahead of him like a labyrinth from which he had no desire to escape; on the contrary he felt an impulse to plunge deeper and deeper into the maze, to take greater and greater risks, to find out its secrets.

But Pompey was concerned only to find food. He found his nest and began to plunder it. He broke one of the eggs to make sure it was fresh, and sucked it up from his hand.

'It's great. Just like a pullet's. I'll have another.'

But before he could do so they heard a new sound—the sound of a field-gate being opened and shut. The game-keeper! Pompey dropped the eggs and they both ran for the wall, the brambles tearing their bare shins and the low twigs scratching their faces. As they were scrambling over the wall they heard somebody shouting after them. Keir expected any second to hear the report of his gun. He had heard that the gamekeeper didn't hesitate to pepper anybody he found trespassing in the park. Some said that he even fired needles out of his gun, and Keir expected at any moment to feel the thin steel sinking into his flesh. But no shot came, and nothing whistled round his head. Only when they had got about a hundred yards beyond the wall they looked back, and saw the keeper with his field-glasses trained on them.

All that day and the next Keir went in fear and trembling of having been seen and recognised and reported; and just when he was beginning to think that the danger was over, he heard his mother say something to one of her neighbours that brought all his fear back.

'They say that young Pompey Allchurch is in trouble again, Hannah. Hev ye heard?'

'Aye. They say the pollis called this mornin', and he has to go up before the juvenile.'

'What's he been up to this time, Hannah?'

'I haven' heard yet, but whativver it is, they winna let him off this time. They'll put him inside, as sure as I'm here.'

'He might get off wi' a fine—though how his mother will find money for a fine dear only knaas. She canna keep that family fed, nivver mind paying fines.'

Pompey's been recognised, thought Keir! My turn next! If the gamekeeper had recognised Pompey he would have recognised his accomplice. Maybe he too would be fined. Maybe he would have to go to prison with Pompey. He went to see if he could find Pompey and ask him what had happened, but he couldn't find him in the street, and he was frightened to go to the house.

He was sitting miserably in his corner in the kitchen when his father came in.

'I hear that young Pompey Allchurch has landed hissel in trouble again.'

'Aye, the pollis was there this mornin'.'

'You would think he'd have mair sense than trying to steal from an old woman, wouldn't ye?'

'What did you say, da?' said Keir, jumping up.

'They say the bobby catched him brikkin' into old Mrs Tinley's shop in Newton Street. Pinching chocolates and sweets.'

'Not pheasants' eggs?'

'Pheasants' eggs! Hes tha tekken leave of thy senses? Mrs Tinley dissent sell pheasants' eggs. Not as far as I know.'

'I meant . . . I meant . . .'

'You've got a guilty look on your face, my lad. Have you been getting yerself mixed up in this?'

'No, da.'

'You'd better not.'

'Well,' said Mrs Ramsay, 'you'd better stop going around wi' that Pompey. He'll finish up in jail, will that one, and he'll have you in the same cell if he gets his own way. Where are you off to now?'

'I want to get a book from Chas,' Keir said, and ran out into the street. He wanted to be by himself, to run and jump and fling his arms about in relief. He had not been seen after all! The dreaded summons was not for him—and he was out of danger once more.

'I wonder what he's been up to,' said Mrs Ramsay, as soon as he had gone. 'I just hope that he hasn't had a hand in this business. 'Cos him and that Pompey's been in each other's pockets for weeks now.'

'Nivver worry about that, hinny. He's a wild lad, and he gets into mischief, but I'll be surprised if he ivver teks anything that isn't his. He didn't look guilty to me. He looked mair like a lad that's had a load lifted off his mind.'

Nevertheless, before Keir was allowed to go to bed, his father gave him a good talking-to.

'It beats me how a lad wi' thy brains canna find somebody better to knock around wi' than that Pompey Allchurch. He's a dead wrong 'un, that lad. So just keep away from him or you'll be the next to get into trouble. That Headmaster of yours is not the kind of feller to keep lads in his school that have been snaffling. You'll be out on your ear, in double quick time. I must say you've picked a good time to get yersels into trouble.'

'I haven't done anything, da.'

'I hope so. God only knaas we hev enough trouble coming to us without your disgracing yerself. So just you keep your nose clean, or else you'll get a taste of Pompey's medicine.'

Whatever medicine Pompey had had to swallow, and there were rumours that his father had 'half-murdered' him, he seemed unrepentant. Before a few days were over he was trying to get Keir to go with him on another raid on the Park. But Keir didn't go with him. He had enough sense to know what his father had meant about his own troubles. Things were not going well at the pit. The owners were determined to make the men accept lower wages and longer hours, and the men were ready to strike rather than give in. The great struggle between masters and men was coming nearer every day.

But there was something else that troubled him. He knew that he hadn't done his best at school. He had played the fool and become known as an idler. He'd never been out of the last six in the form. He'd never had any desire to be higher. He had never felt any special loyalty to anyone, except perhaps Mr Howard, but he realised now, almost for the first time, that the last thing he wanted was to be disgraced and expelled.

SEVEN

Major Goldie

Before the week was out Keir's father had a stroke of bad luck. Usually at the end of his shift he took his watch out of his pit waistcoat and hung it on the 'bradish', but for once he left it in. While he was getting bathed in front of the fire, his wife picked up his pit-clothes, as she always did, and took them out to 'dad' them—that is to knock the coal dust out of them by beating them against the wall. As soon as he heard the thump-thump of the clothes being 'dadded', he remembered that his watch was still in the waistcoat pocket and called out to her to stop. It was too late. The clothes had been thumped so hard that not only was the glass shattered but all the pointers had dropped off. 'Lad, thoo's the clumsiest woman I've ivver seen in all my born days. If there's owt to be broken you'll break it,' he said.

'Be fair, Geordie. Be fair. It's not my job to tek the watch out. It's not my fault if tha's got a memory like a sieve.'

'Why, one thing's certain. I canna manage without a watch. I'll have to pop into Durham th' morn and see if I can get a cheap one in the market.'

The following afternoon he and Keir walked into the city. Mr Ramsay bought himself a watch from one of the stalls in the covered market. When they were coming out Keir noticed that the doors of the Town Hall were open, and on the steps leading up to the door there was a notice

'MODEL TRAIN EXHIBITION ADMISSION FREE'

He had never been inside the Town Hall. It was there that the school held its Speech Days, but space was very limited and only prizewinners and their parents were allowed to attend. Keir had never won a prize for anything. This was the first chance he had had of seeing what it was like inside the Hall.

It was a high narrow place with a lofty ceiling like the ceiling of a church. The windows were of stained glass, and coats of arms and lists of famous names were painted on the panels on the walls. All round the walls were screens with photographs of old engines and trains and a picture of the opening of the first railway from Darlington to Stockton, like the illustration in a history book he had seen in the library.

The centre of the room was taken up by a big board that had been laid over eight or nine small tables that had been pushed together and covered with a green baize cloth. Along the edges of the board ran a model railway track with sidings, toy stations, signals and signal boxes and even bridges and tunnels; and inside the outer track there was a second, twisted into the shape of a figure of eight. Round the tracks went careering passenger trains, goods trains and a beautiful foreign-looking train with WAGON LITS painted on its sides. On a high stool, at the far side of the table, with his fingers on the control switches, sat a man whom Keir had never expected to see there. It was Major Goldie.

'I don't want to stop here, da,' said Keir, backing out.

'What's up? First of all you break your neck to get in and then you break it to get out.'

'That's Major Goldie sitting on the stool.'

'So it is! The one that talks about the Abolition of Slavery, isn't it?'

'How do you know him?'

'Not many union men that dinna ken him. He's nae friend of ours, is that feller. Lad, I nivver knew he liked playing wi' trains.'

'Don't talk so loudly, da. He'll hear us.'

'I dinna care a damn if he hears us or not,' said Mr Ramsay, more loudly than ever.

The Major must have heard him. He looked up, and whether it was the glimpse he had of Keir trying to hide himself in the crowd, or, what was more likely, the sight of the contemptuous look on Mr Ramsay's face, he fumbled with his switch, and one of his trains swerved, cannoning into and derailing a second train. The crowd laughed, but the Major kept his head and brought everything to a standstill. Then he put the trains on the right tracks and started them up again, but not before he had shot an angry look at Keir and his father, whom he clearly considered the cause of the accident.

As soon as he could Keir pulled his father away. 'Steady on, lad, steady on,' said Mr Ramsay. 'Dinna let him think we're running away from him. There's nae need to be frightened of him. Playing wi' trains at his age, like a bairn! He should be ashamed of hissel.'

EIGHT

The Lock-out

It was Friday evening. Keir was busy with his homework. He usually left it to the last minute, but he wasn't allowed now to go out with Pompey. He thought he would start on his essay. He wrote the title and the date in the right hand corner. Mr Bowles was the only teacher who made you put the date on your homework. It couldn't have mattered much because none of the other teachers bothered about it. But Mr Bowles was very fussy and the first thing he looked for was the date.

All the Friday night callers had come and gone and Keir's mother was sitting cutting up some old clothes into long strips and dropping them into a carrier bag. When the material was soft she impatiently let the scissors rip down through it without closing them. Keir kept looking at her wondering when she was going to stop and get his father's pit clothes out of the cupboard. Mr Ramsay always went in to work early on Saturday morning so that he could finish his shift by dinner time. He used to get the caller to call him just before three in the morning. Keir knew that as soon as his mother began to get out the pit clothes it would be time for him to clear the table for supper. It would be a relief because the essay topic was 'Honesty is the Best Policy' and he couldn't think of a word to say.

But his mother made no move and went on running her scissors down the lengths of material. She was getting her 'clippings' ready for a mat she was making.

'Isn't my da going to work tomorrow, ma?'

'No. He isn't. Naebody is.'

'Are they coming out on strike?'

'No. It's a lock-out. The bosses are locking them out.'

'What's a lock-out?'

'The bosses are shutting the pit. They winna let the men go down.'

'What for?'

'Here's your da. He'll tell you.'

At that moment Mr Ramsay came in. He banged the door shut after him roughly and angrily.

'For heaven's sake, dinna clash the door, Davy,' said his wife.

'Why are the bosses shutting the pit, da?'

'Because they want us to tek a reduction, that's why. And we've refused.'

'A reduction in pay?'

'That's it. Lad, they must think we're flats. Work longer hours and get less? Nivver! But they winna get away wi' it this time, bonny lad. They're starting wi' a lock-out and they'll end up wi' a strike. Afore the week's out ivverybody in the country will be out on strike. Not just us—railwaymen, bus-drivers, shipyard workers—ivverybody.'

'Teachers as well?'

'No, not teachers. But all the working-men in the country will down tools in a few days. There's gonna be a big bust-up, lad. A General Strike. And that'll make Mr Baldwin put his thinking cap on.'

The next day, Saturday, the first of May, every colliery in England, Scotland and Wales was idle. On Monday Keir saw in the *Northern Echo* that Tuesday's paper would be the last to appear until further notice. The TUC had called for a General Strike to begin on Wednesday, the fourth of May.

PART TWO

The Nine Days

ONE

The First Day of the Strike

Keir usually set off for school as soon as the eight o'clock buzzer had gone, but there was no buzzer this morning. An extraordinary silence had fallen over the whole colliery. There were no tankies fussing up and down the sidings, no sound of trucks being shunted, no sound of hammering from the workshops. No smoke came from the high pit chimney, and the pulley wheels were at a standstill. As he and Chas walked down the hill towards the Durham road they saw the little engine that took the men up to the drifts on Hassop Hill standing in its siding. There was no driver or stoker on the footplate, no fire burning under the boiler.

A mile further on they came to the main road and passed under the silent viaduct. Nine times out of ten they saw the London–Edinburgh express thundering along this stretch of line, but nothing came and the signals never moved. The signal cabin at the end of the viaduct was empty. There were more people on the road now, clerks who worked in the Shirehall at Durham, shop-assistants, women who cleaned hotels, and served in the cafés and bars. Pa Walcott—the Head—passed them in his Trojan, its solid rubber wheels making a drumming noise as it rumbled past. He must have gone out of his way to pick up some of the teachers. Mr Smelley was with him, looking very smug and superior.

Assembly was only half-full. No train boys—either the boys from Eshaw and Cornhope, or the Scorburn boys—had arrived; and for once there was room to breathe in the Assembly Hall. There were no more than half-a-dozen prefects standing along the wall at the side of the hall. Mr Hutchinson, who usually played the organ at 'Assem', hadn't turned up yet, and Mr Smelley took his place, but he made a terrible mess of the tunes, hitting all the wrong notes and throwing everybody wrong. Once he didn't notice that they had come to the end of the hymn and struck up again, but when he found nobody was singing he stopped, and the organ gave a groan as if it wanted to tell everybody how much it was suffering. Pa Walcott made no mention of the strike. He went through the service as he always did, snorting as he read that lesson he was never tired of repeating:

Wherewithal shall a young man cleanse his ways?

When they went back to their rooms for lessons some of the classes found to their delight that there was nobody to take them. Six masters had still not turned up—Mr Hutchinson, Mr Gladwell, Mr Wright, . . . and Major Goldie. Even the teachers who had turned up didn't seem anxious to begin, but stood in groups discussing the strike, till Pa Walcott came out of his study with his watch in his hand and made them hop. Just after half-past-nine those classes that had no teacher were told to muster in the Hall. By this time Mr Hutchinson had arrived and he took them all for a hymn practice (the Head must have been disgusted with their performance in 'Assem'). Then Mr Howard brought in his gramophone and a pile of records, and for half an hour he played them some classical music, stopping to explain how the music was put together. Keir liked that.

At ten, Mr Howard took Keir and the rest of his form off to the North School—to their form-room in the North

School—for Latin. Nearly half the desks were empty, but Mr Howard took the lesson as he always did, drilling them in their conjugations and declensions and getting their brains working. Then he stopped, and gave them a passage from De Bello Gallico to work through on their own. They could use the glossary at the back and any notes they could find.

A few moments after they had started the room fell very quiet, and there was no noise except the turning over of leaves and the scratching of pens on the pages of the exercise books. Keir, who was sitting near a window, looked up once and saw a girl in a house opposite come into the room, pick up a baby and shove a dummy into its mouth. She took as little notice of Keir as he did of her.

Then he became aware of another sound, the clip-clopping of a pony on the cobbles of the street below him, and the trundling, not of one of the common carts that rag-and-bone men brought up South Street, but of something lighter. He saw Mr Howard get up from his desk, walk over to the window and break into a smile.

'Pens down, everybody! I want you to come over to the windows—not too fast now, not in a mad rush—there now, there's something you won't forget in a hurry, I hope.'

It was Mr Frogmore the Art Master. He was sitting bolt upright on the seat of a gig, dressed in his fawn coloured suit with the high lapels, a straw hat on his head and a buttonhole in his coat. Beside him sat his driver, a bullet-headed old man whom Keir had never seen before. As he sat there with his gold pince-nez glinting in the sunlight Mr Frogmore looked —not like a teacher reporting for duty—but an elegant French gentleman on a visit to some distinguished friend.

'Well done, Mr Frogmore!' shouted Mr Howard, leaning out of the window. 'You're arriving in style. Give Mr Frogmore a round of applause, boys.'

'Hooray, hooray, hooray,' shouted the boys. It wasn't often

they were actually encouraged to make a noise in their classroom, and they made the most of the opportunity. Mr Frogmore, lifting his straw hat, stepped out of his gig and waved to them in acknowledgment of their cheers.

'Now that's something you won't forget, boys,' said Mr Howard, 'a true English gentleman who means to do his duty whatever obstacles may be put in his way. All right. Back to your desks now. You have five minutes to finish your translation.' 'Back to the Calico Belly,' said Keir's neighbour. If Mr Howard heard him, he ignored the comment.

Before the morning was over a few more of the missing teachers arrived, but Major Goldie never turned up, and instead of History Keir's form were allowed to do their homework. Mr Smelley supervised the lesson. He was in a filthy mood. He had been cock-a-hoop when the Head gave him a lift, but he hadn't got over the mess he made of the hymns at 'Assem'.

'Don't you boys think that because the train boys are allowed to stay away from school the same applies to you! Strike or no strike you're expected at school and anybody using the strike as an excuse will catch it from me personally. Got that?'

But he could find no one boy to vent his mortification on.

Everyone thought that Pa Walcott would let them all go home early, but they were disappointed. He didn't let them go till the cathedral bell had struck four. But it didn't matter much because most of the boys had done their homework in the unexpected free periods, and the satchels they carried home that day were light.

A strange thing happened in Hassop that night, something that had not happened since that famous day in 1918 when the Armistice was declared. You would have thought that another war had been fought and won. And so in a way it had—for the men of the Bishop Pit. Not a single man had gone to work. The strike was complete and Keir's father was full of news. The strike was a great success. The railwaymen all over the country were out—the bus drivers and the men in the shipyards, and so on, and so on. The bandsmen put on their uniforms and gave an impromptu concert in the village square. When they had come to the end of their set pieces they began to play dances, and men and women came out to dance in the square. When it was all over they stayed out in the streets. One man brought out a concertina and they all sat on the steps outside their houses listening and talking. Nobody seemed to want to go to bed. As the light went out of the sky they sat on talking until almost midnight.

Only when it grew too cold to sit out any more did the jubilant people begin to go in. When Keir went to bed he could still hear the concertina player playing on and on in the darkness.

TWO

The Second Day

On Wednesday, the second day of the strike, there were more people than ever on the road to the city. Hardly anybody from the colliery worked there, but once Keir had joined the main Durham road he met a steady stream of people from the village and from Hilton, farther along the main road. Those who had waited in vain on Tuesday for trains and buses now realised that if they were to get to work in time they would have to get there under their own steam. Many were on cycles, and one elderly man who worked in a shop in Silver Street had even brought out an old tricycle. From time to time a car went past, every seat taken. In one, two girls had been squashed into a tiny dickey seat at the back of a Morris Oxford. But most were on foot, and the nearer they got to the city the thicker the file of walkers grew. Half way to the city they came across a bus that had broken down. Neither the blackleg driver nor the soldier who had been detailed to protect him could do anything to get the bus going. They stood looking helplessly at the engine and the jet of steam coming from the radiator One of the side windows of the bus had been broken—and it had been boarded up with plywood on which some wag had chalked

'I have no pane now, Mother dear.'

Most of the passengers had got out and decided to finish the journey on foot.

The Headmaster's car went rattling past them again, with Mr Smelley looking a little crestfallen after his fiasco at the organ; and as they were going down the long hill into the city Keir saw Mr Howard striding down on the opposite side of the road enjoying, as he always did, his early morning walk in the clear air.

Mr Hutchinson was still not in 'Assem' but Mr Smelley was not asked to play the organ in his place.

'Dropped!' whispered Harry Needham who was standing next to Keir. 'Dropped after one game! He looks as black as thunder.'

Mr Smelley looked surly and displeased, and the performance of Mr Wright, who took his place, did not make him any happier. The second choice went through the service without one mistake.

This time the Head didn't read a lesson from the Psalms. Instead, he spoke to them about the strike. 'There is no need for me to tell you what happened yesterday and has continued to happen today. The country is going through a grave crisis. I'm not going to speak to you about the rights and the wrongs of this dispute. What I want to say is that I don't want any of you to get the idea that because there is a General Strike you can use that as an excuse for slacking. I understand that some of the boys who have to rely on trains are not at school. They will be excused from attendance—but nobody else will. The rest of the country may be laying down its tools but work goes on at this school as it has always gone on. And anybody caught playing the fool will be dealt with . . .'

The Head had spoken about 'business as usual' at school, but there was more confusion than he knew; and it didn't take Keir long to realise that anybody who wished to play the fool could get away with a great deal. There were not enough prefects or masters to do yard-duty properly. It was a school rule that only those boys who lived in the city were allowed to leave the school premises during the dinner hour, unless special permission was given. It had always been easy to slip out. The difficulty was sneaking back, because once dinner was over there was always someone posted at the end of the entrance tunnel that you had to report to.

But Keir had already noticed on Tuesday that there was nobody on duty. It was a golden opportunity to get out and see what was happening in the city.

As soon as they had eaten their sandwiches, Keir and Harry Needham escaped through the tunnel and got clear of South Street without being noticed. They crossed Framwellgate Bridge and walked up Silver Street. Normally Silver Street was busy and dangerous. The buses went up and down it, and at the cry 'There's a bus comin'!' shoppers would have to crowd on to the narrow pavements. But now there were no buses, and hardly any shoppers to be jostled on to the pavements. Keir saw the old man who had ridden in on his tricycle standing at the door of the outfitters' shop where he worked. The shop was empty. A little further on another cautious shopkeeper was nailing planks across his shop windows. All the shopkeepers had planks ready for the big Miners Gala in July. They nailed them across the shop fronts to keep windows from being pushed in by the crowds. Keir wondered if the man was expecting some kind of riot. But Silver Street was quiet and silent and almost empty.

There were more people in the Market Place. A big convoy of lorries labelled ESSENTIAL SUPPLIES had stopped there, and a small company of soldiers in uniform guarded the lorries. Those on duty were standing around the lorries with fixed bayonets; but the rest were lounging on the steps around the statue in the market-place, smoking and playing cards.

Then suddenly a man with a red flag jumped up on to the topmost step of the plinth and began to make some kind of speech to the soldiers, and to any one else who cared to listen to him. Keir could hear only scraps of what he said—'Comrades . . . ashamed of yourselves . . . join in the battle with your working class comrades . . . don't let them turn you into blacklegs . . . help your fellow-workers to gain a decent wage . . .' Keir listened with only half an ear. He was more interested in a policeman who was standing next to him. He had taken out a notebook and was jotting down what the speaker was saying. Then when he had taken down enough, he snapped his notebook closed and went up to the speaker.

'I'm arresting you,' he said. 'I'm arresting you for sedition. You're trying to prevent the King's men from carrying out their lawful duty. So you'd better come quiet. Are you coming, or have I to fetch you?'

The man continued to wave his flag and to try to address the soldiers. But the policeman blew his whistle, and Keir saw that in the far corner of the square there was a Black Maria. Two constables jumped out and between them they hustled the man into the van and drove away. Keir saw one of the soldiers, who had stood by and watched the scene, pick up the red flag that had fallen to the ground. He threw it in the air and it landed across the arm of the figure of the Duke on the statue.

'Hey, look at that! I've turned the Duke hissel into a Bolshie,' he shouted. 'Bet he never thought he'd be waving the red flag!'

The clock in the church in the corner of the square struck two. Turning, Keir and his pal ran down Silver Street and just managed to get into their places before the teacher came in.

That night Keir listened to his wireless, trying to get the

Savoy Orpheans again. When he heard the announcer say that the Prime Minister, Mr Baldwin, was going to make a statement, he shouted to his father and asked him if wanted to listen.

'Ye canna believe a word he says,' said Mr Ramsay, 'but I'll listen.'

They took an ear-phone each, and Keir heard the Prime Minister speaking.

'*The General Strike,* he said, *is an operation expressing in no uncertain terms a direct challenge to ordered government . . . an effort to force upon some 42 million British citizens the will of less than 4 million others engaged in the vital services of the country. The strike is a direct hold-up of the nation to ransom. . . .*'

But Keir didn't want to listen to any more. He left his father trying to fit the other earphone over his head, and went out to find Pompey.

THREE

The Third Day

Major Goldie had still not returned to school. Nor had any of the train boys except one sixth former from Eshaw who got a lift on a motor-bike every day. If anything, there were less prefects on duty than ever, and at dinner time Keir and Harry slipped out again to see what was happening in the city. A few more buses were on the move, and most of the blackleg drivers had a soldier or a policeman sitting beside them to protect them. One bus had barbed wire wrapped round the bonnet to stop anyone tampering with the engine. But the market place looked emptier than ever. The convoy had moved on and the soldiers with it. Outside a newsagent's shop there was a big poster with

'*Strikers begin to Weaken*
Drift back to Work'

but the market square was almost deserted. The policeman in the traffic kiosk had hardly anything to do. Somebody had removed the red flag from the statue of the Duke.

At the bottom of Claypath there was a wireless shop that sold coils, earphones, condensers etc. Keir and Harry spent some time looking at the things in the window. There was no chance of their being able to buy anything, but Keir liked to look at the new equipment he would have bought had he been better off. Then they went down to the riverside. They could easily walk along the banks to Framwellgate Bridge and then to school.

When they came to Prebends Bridge they saw a college crew practising on the river. They were doing practice starts. There was a big notice saying 'DANGER—WEIR', but the oarsmen kept going dangerously near to the weir then sprinting away from it. Then another boat came shooting the big arch of Prebends and it looked for a moment as if there was going to be a collision.

Keir and Harry were so absorbed that they forgot the time till they heard the cathedral bell begin to strike two. But they were not worried because the first lesson of the afternoon was History and Major Goldie wouldn't be there to take it, and whoever came in to take the lesson wouldn't know who was supposed to be there and who wasn't. They could easily slip in at the end of the first lesson and nobody would be the wiser.

'Who took you for History?' he asked the boy who sat next to him, when he had managed to sneak into the classroom.

'Smelley.'

'What did he do?'

'He took us for extra Geometry. And do you know what he said? He said, "You should have History homework but you're going to get Geometry instead."'

'When is it for?'

'Tomorrow.'

'Are we going to have him again?'

'Yes.'

'Oh God! What's the homework?'

'Problems. On page . . . sh! Here's Nobby Bowles. I'll tell you later.'

But Keir forgot to ask again, and it was only when he got home and was starting on his homework that he remembered he had still not found out exactly which problems they had to do. Never mind, Chas would know. Chas always knew what they had to do. He left his books on the table and set out for Windsor Gardens.

It was Mr Futers who answered the door. He didn't have his green eye-shade on this time, and he looked tired and cross.

'You here again? What do you want this time?'

'I wanted to ask Chas if he could tell me what problems we have to do in Geometry.'

'Well it's no good coming here. He's out at Choir Practice.'

'Has he done his homework?'

'Of course he's done it. He does that first thing—and so would you if you had any sense. 'Procrastination is the thief of time'. You've heard that before, haven't you?'

Keir had heard it many times before—and from the same lips that uttered it now.

'Can I have a look at his book, Mr Futers?'

'So you can copy it? Not likely!'

'Can I look at his Geometry text book and see which ones he's marked? What we have to do?'

'Lad, you're the biggest nuisance in Hassop. Always wanting, wanting, wanting. Do you think I have time to start looking for things like that at this time of night?'

But in spite of all his grumbling he went back into the house and came back with the book in his hand.

'This is the last time, mind. Page 66, and the ones he's marked are numbers 6 and 7. Can you keep that in your head?'

'Thanks very much, Mr Futers. Page 66. Number 6 and number 7.'

'Good job for you it's easy to remember, isn't it?'

'Yes. Thanks very much, Mr Futers.'

Before he could finish the door was shut against him. He

didn't mind. He had found out what he wanted to know.

He found the problems very difficult. They didn't seem to have much connection with what they had been doing, but maybe this was the work they had been doing while he and Harry had been enjoying themselves looking at the rowing. He struggled through them and did them, after a fashion.

When he had finished he went into the Room to listen to his wireless. The Announcer was speaking about some riots that had broken out in Glasgow. But more trains, he said, were in service, and thousands of patriotic citizens were helping to keep buses and trains running. There were signs that the strike was weakening and that everything would be back to normal within a few days. The Archbishop of Canterbury was going to make a special appeal to the country on Friday.

Keir was not very interested. He kept hoping that the Savoy Orpheans would come on the air. And soon he heard them being announced and starting with his favourite tune

'Ain't no sense
Sitting on the fence
All by yourself in the moonlight
Ain't no fun
Sitting all alone
Giving yourself a hug
Giving yourself a squeeze. . . .'

FOUR

The Fourth Day

'Right. Put your homework open on the desk in front of you, and I'll come round and check it.'

Mr Smelley began to walk quickly up and down the aisles ticking the work as he went. Keir knew from the speed at which he was going that all he was looking at were the constructions. Keir wasn't altogether happy about the way he had worked out the problems, but he felt fairly sure about his constructions. He looked idly round him waiting for Mr Smelley to enter his red ticks and move on. But he didn't move on. Instead he bent down, picked up the exercise book and began to look at it closely.

'What's this supposed to be?'

'My homework, sir.'

'What on earth have you been up to? Who told you to do these problems?'

'You did, sir.'

'You ass! You've done the wrong ones. Every boy in the class does the right ones—but you have to be different, haven't you? Who has the detention sheet?'

'I have, sir,' said Chas.

'Detention for you, Ramsay, you chump. How did you manage to get the wrong problems when the rest of the class understood me perfectly well?'

'I thought, sir, I thought. . . .'

'Yes, you're always thinking, but you don't think the right things. Report to Mr Frogmore at four sharp tonight.'

All the boys stood in awe of Pa Walcott. He was not a cruel headmaster, and to tell the truth Keir had never known anyone get a caning from him. He was always known as Pa—that was his only nickname. But he was so remote and awesome a figure that no one was ever summoned to his study without feeling that he was being called upon to face a stern and unrelenting judge. Even the most hardened rebel and wrongdoer quaked as he heard the big oaken door close after him, and found himself standing in front of the Head's wide leather-topped desk. Yet few boys were ever expelled. Pa's favourite punishment was detention.

The detention class was always held in the Physics Lab., and you had to sit on stools at the long lab. benches. You were not supposed to do anything—no talking, no reading, no homework—but if you were cunning you could look at a book on your knee or pass messages from one to another. Sometimes Pa himself would come in and look round, like an ogre weighing up which victim he would choose next for sacrifice.

Keir looked up at the clock that hung on the wall behind Mr Frogmore's head. The hands moved so slowly you would have thought they had stopped. He looked away from the clock and tried to make out the half-erased formula on the blackboard

$$x = + \text{ or } - (a + b)(a - b) - 4 \ldots$$

He stared for a moment through the high windows at the empty sky, at the gas tap of the Bunsen burner on the bench, the inside of the sink. Then as he looked up he noticed that Mr Frogmore had picked up his newspaper and was holding it up. The newspaper was *The British Gazette*, a name that

Keir had never seen before, and there was a big headline

'Workers' Resistance Crumbling
11000 Special Constables Sworn in'

Keir leaned forward to see if he could read the smaller print, but at that moment Mr Frogmore laid the paper flat again, and he could see no more.

Bored and restless, he fumbled in his bag and pulled out a sheet of paper with a poem written on it. It was a poem that they had been given to learn by Tug Wilson the Geography master. It seemed a daft thing to do, to have to learn a poem for Geography, but they had been doing the Savannahs of Africa and Tug had been talking about trees like the baobab, and he'd made them copy out this poem. Keir spread out the poem on his knee and showed it to the boy who was next to him—Alan Nattrass who was in the same form.

The poem started

'*Creek, creek, that's the pulai*' (you had to pronounce it so that it rhymed with 'sigh')

'*Its bole arock with brisk-blown breezes. . . .*'

When Mr Frogmore wasn't looking, Alan passed a note to Keir

'*Creek, creek, that's my glass-eye,*
It pops out every time I sneezes . . .'

Keir could hardly stop himself from giggling, but at that moment Mr Frogmore picked up his paper again, turned it over and looked straight past it at the boys, who immediately assumed an air of immense innocence.

Now that Mr Frogmore had turned over the paper Keir could see a second headline

'Archbishop Appeals—Resume Work Now
Prime Minister Confident'

Keir leant forward again to see if he could read more, but Mr Frogmore suddenly shook his paper, folded it and said, 'How many of you boys have to walk home?'

They all put up their hands—even Alan Nattrass who, as

everybody knew, came to school on his bike. 'All right. These are not normal times. I am going to end the detention period now. You can all go, but go quietly, and don't draw attention to yourselves.'

Friday night was always a busy night in the colliery for Friday night was pay night, even though it was on this occasion only strike pay. This was the night on which the weekly pay was received—and, in the main, spent. There was a constant coming and going of callers—the insurance man, a foxy-faced little man with a red toothbrush moustache, whom Keir could never take to (even his mother called him a 'smarmy little beggar'); the slick man from the Co-op with his order book and the carbon paper that Keir envied, reciting at great speed all the wonderful items he had to offer—tapioca, semolina, Scott's Emulsion, ground rice, self-raising flour, butter (best butter it always was), margarine, essence of lemon, yeast, bacon, eggs, boiled ham, tongue, polony . . . ticking them and whipping out his carbon paper in readiness for the next customer; Doggart's Club man for his weekly contribution; the sanctimonious butcher who was also a local preacher, with the scales swinging from the back of his cart and a retinue of mongrels behind him, ready to snap up any scrag-end thrown down to them; and finally poor Cyril Futers with his two huge suitcases that he was condemned to lug around with him from house to house, crammed with cheap blouses, packets of pins, spotted handkerchieves, flannel pit shirts, ribbons and socks. Keir never thought of him without these two battered suitcases that he seemed doomed to carry around with him for ever, like a convict's ball and chain.

There was a mystery about poor Cyril. Somewhere, at some time, he had committed some unknown sin, had lost his job (had he, too, embezzled the chapel funds somewhere?) and had been taken on by his brother, Chas's father. Keir heard his father and mother say from time to time, 'Poor Cyril, that brother of his has made him pay for that little slip of his. He meks a packet out of him, that he does. He meks a mint out of him, but treats him like a dog. He's a proper slave.'

So Cyril carried around with him his two heavy cases like the symbols of his crime, but the women of the colliery were good to him, and Mrs Ramsay would never let him go without buying something from him, however small.

In normal times there was always some treat for Keir on Friday—a tin of pineapple chunks, or a quarter of custard creams. But there were few delicacies that night for anybody in the colliery; and many was the house where the insurance man and the club man and even poor Cyril went away empty-handed.

When all the callers had come and gone Keir went into the Room to listen in for a few minutes. He hoped that he might hear a jazz band playing, but all he could get was someone talking about the Strike. He was pleading with the men to go back to work, and for the Government to tell the miners that they would not have to take a cut in wages. He was just going to turn off when the speaker ended, and he heard an announcer saying, 'You have just been listening to His Grace the Archbishop of Canterbury speaking to the country on this the fourth day of the General Strike. Later this evening the Prime Minister, the Right Honourable Stanley Baldwin, will speak on behalf of the Government; but first there will be a programme of light music given by the Savoy Havana Band.' He sat listening to the band, fiddling with his cat's whisker trying to find a better spot on the crystal until he heard the announcer introducing the Prime Minister. He didn't want to listen to a speech. He turned the set off and went to bed. He looked through some of his old comics for a few minutes, then got up and put out the light, and fell asleep.

FIVE

The Fifth Day

Keir knew that it was best for him to keep out of his mother's way on Saturday mornings. The time between breakfast and dinner was given up to putting the house straight for the weekend, and that meant taking up the weekday mats, shaking them and putting them away, scrubbing the floor, bath-bricking the hearth, and polishing the best fender, tidy and fire-irons. Anyone who got in his mother's way while she was busy with these jobs got short shrift.

Keir hadn't done his homework yet—that was not unusual because he always put it off till the last minute. It was out of the question to try to start now, so he went outside to find somebody to play with. His father had gone off to meet his mates and go for a walk with them through the fields. They would finish up at the Club. Mr Ramsay had given up most of his pocket-money, but he still had enough for a gill. Most of the men were content if they had just enough to get them into the Club. Then they could sit and play cards and dominoes as long as they wished.

Soon after twelve, they both came back to find the house spick and span, smelling of metal polish and bath-brick.

'Have ye heard the news, Lizzie?' asked Mr Ramsay.

'What, is the strike off?'

'Nay. That'll nivver be off till the bosses give in. No, it's not that. They say somebody's been damaging the railway line down at Smallburn.'

'Nivver!'

'Aye. They're trying to stop the London trains from getting to Newcastle.'

'Well, strike or nae strike, I dinna hold with a trick like that. There could be a nasty accident. Who did it?'

'Naebody seems to knaa. But they say they're sending a gang of blacklegs to mend the line. They'll get a rough reception if they try that.'

'Well, just you keep away.'

'What, and let blacklegs get away wi' it? There'll be half Hassop down there this afternoon.'

'It would be mair menseful for you to keep away. Ye dinna want to get mixed up with any mair trouble. You knaa what it's like. You're such a hot-headed feller you're sure to be the one to get caught.'

Nothing she could say had any effect on her husband. As soon as he had had his dinner he pulled on his coat and went out. Keir followed him, and Jimmy—who had appeared from nowhere—followed Keir. Keir hated being seen going around with a boy smaller than himself—nobody made friends with boys in lower forms—but now that Pompey wasn't there to go with him, he was better disposed towards Jimmy. They set off together for the railway cutting at Smallburn.

When they came to the embankment overlooking the cutting they saw some twenty or thirty men already at work there, levering into position the lengths of track that had been damaged, and hammering in the wooden chocks that kept the rails in place. They were not dressed like workmen, but wore cricket sweaters, open-necked shirts, tweed jackets and shoes. There was one man with a pair of pinstriped trousers, like the ones Mr Futers wore, tucked into his socks, and another wearing gloves. They seemed to be enjoying the work and every now and then someone would burst out laughing. A few hundred yards down the line the passenger train that had been brought to a stop fumed and hissed, a thin column of smoke twisting out of the funnel. The men from Hassop looked down on the men and the train with troubled, angry faces.

Although the gang was still working on the track the driver of the waiting train began to whistle impatiently and to edge his train forward, but when it came close to the damaged length of track someone flagged it down. Keir heard the carriages cannoning together as the brakes went on, and saw the driver and his mate climb down out of the cab. They were wearing peaked caps, long trench coats and big gloves. As they appeared the men on the embankment, who had been quiet up to that moment, broke into angry shouting.

'Blacklegs! Dirty blacklegs!'

'Get back to yer own jobs!'

'Get yersels back to where ye belang!'

There was a man standing close to Keir—it was a man called Tommy Blenkinsop, a man who had once worked marras with his father—and Keir saw him bend down, pick up a stone and fling it at the train driver. It missed him, but it hit the boiler of the engine with a queer clanging noise; and the sound seemed to release the pent-up anger of the men. More and more stones and clods were thrown. Most of the blacklegs treated the attack contemptuously at first, ducking and using their shovels like cricket bats, but when one or two had been hit they began to give ground. Now all the strikers armed themselves, and Keir, who was never slow to join in a fight, picked up a stone for himself. He had just drawn his arm back to throw it when he saw something hit the back of the driver in the trench coat. The man turned round sharply and his eyes lit on Keir, who was standing with his arm upraised. For a moment the boy and the man looked straight at each other—and Keir saw that the man into whose eyes he was looking was Major Goldie.

Then all around him there was a cry—'The pollis, the pollis!' Looking round, he saw a bus pull up on the side of the road near the cutting, and helmeted policemen with truncheons drawn clamber out and run across the field. He dropped his stone and ran, with Jimmy after him, along the side of the embankment till they came to a clump of gorse bushes not far from a level crossing. They flung themselves down, listening to the sound of pursued and pursuers dying away.

A few minutes later they heard the whistle of the train. A jet of white smoke shot up into the air, and one by one the carriages were jerked forward. As the train drew close Keir could see the passengers leaning out of the windows and waving triumphantly at a silent group of men and women at the level crossing. Keir shrank back out of sight. He didn't want Major Goldie to see him again.

'Well,' said Mr Ramsay, when he came in that night. 'That teacher of yours has got what he wanted after all.'

'What's that, da?'

'He always wanted to drive a train, didn' he? Now he's got his chance. I hope he manages it better than he did that toy train we saw him playing wi'. If he dissent, God help his passengers.'

SIX

The Sixth Day

Keir hadn't yet looked at his homework, but he began to think that he had already got into one scrape and it wouldn't be wise to get into another. When his mother started peeling the taties, and stripping off the bad cabbage leaves and filling pans and steamers for the Sunday dinner he went into the Room and took out his books. He tried to memorise a poem from Mount Helicon that Nobby Bowles the English master had told them to learn, but the words wouldn't stick. He put on his earphones and began to fiddle with his cat's whisker. It didn't sound as if there was anything on the air because all he heard were crackles and hisses. He was glad when he heard the voice of Tommy Gill in the kitchen.

Tommy Gill was the paper-man, and he took the Sunday papers round himself. He always stopped for a 'crack' when he came to the Ramsays. He dropped his heavy bag of papers on the floor, lit his pipe and settled down for a few minutes.

'That was a queer carry-on down at the cut yesterday, Davy,' he said.

'Aye. It would ha' been queerer still if the pollis han't arrived on the scene.'

'They tell me they took a few names. Young Albert Jackson and Nick Turnbull both got their names took. They say they'll be up for assault or breach of the peace or summat like that.'

'They didn't dee a thing.'

'Maybe not, but they'll be up in court for all that. And the pollis hev a few mair names in their books. There'll be a tidy few mair will be getting a summons afore they're finished.'

'They'll nivver be able to mek up a case against them.'

'I hope not. But ye knaa what the bobbies is like nowadays. The mair they can bring up the better for them. That's the way to get promotion these days.'

Keir didn't mean to listen to this conversation. He had come into the kitchen to see if there was a story in the paper that he would like to read. Every week there was a detective story by Edgar Wallace and Keir had read them all. But as he heard Mr Gill talking he forgot about the story. If the police had been taking names, maybe they had taken his. He was sure that Major Goldie had recognised him. What would happen if he had given Keir's name to the police? He went back into the Room and tried once more to concentrate. In the end he gave it up, and went out to seek somebody to play with.

After dinner his father took the paper up to bed with him. Strike or no strike, most of the men in Hassop spent Sunday afternoon in bed with the paper. Mrs Ramsay settled in front of the fire in her rocking chair and prepared to drop off for a few minutes. Keir finished his homework at last, then fiddled with his wireless set till tea-time. He was still feeling restless and the sound of footsteps coming down the street agitated him. As soon as tea was over he got ready to go to chapel. He made up his mind that if Jimmy Metcalf was going he would go with him.

Mr and Mrs Ramsay never went either to chapel or church, but Keir sometimes went to the evening service on Sunday because he liked to go to the Mount Calvary 'socials', and you couldn't get in if you didn't belong to the chapel.

By the time he got there the chapel was nearly full, but he could see that Jimmy had kept a seat for him near the front. He would rather have stayed at the back but he could see that Jimmy was wanting him to join him.

While he was waiting for the service to begin he sat looking up at the big wooden pulpit above him. Hanging down from the pulpit desk was a kind of banner with the letters IHS sewn on it. Once he had thought that the letters meant In His Service, but one day Mr Howard had told him that it was really Latin and stood for Jesu Hominum Salvator and the first letter I was really a J. Behind the pulpit sat the choir on tiered seats like the seats in the big stand at St James's Park at Newcastle. He could see Isaac Moss sitting well towards the front. There was something wrong with Isaac's neck and it didn't fit properly on to his shoulders, but that didn't stop him from being a good singer and he always took a solo part when the chapel did an oratorio. Keir's father said he could have made a fortune with his voice if he had had anybody to back him.

On the big bare walls behind the choir there was a text painted in red letters on a kind of wavy scroll

Vengeance is Mine, saith the Lord. I will repay.

Keir wasn't much frightened of the Lord, but he couldn't help thinking of the policeman that even at that moment might be knocking on his door in Stephenson Street.

The door of the vestry opened and the preacher began to mount the steps to the pulpit. Keir had seen him before. He was a man from Cornhope, well-known for his long-winded sermons. He had a habit of using long sentences and giving or delivering them all without taking a breath, so that he got redder and redder and more and more breathless before he came to the end of the sentence. As soon as he saw him Keir knew that they were in for a long service. Well, the longer the better. So long as he was in chapel he was safe. No one could hand you a summons when you were in chapel. It was like being in sanctuary.

After the hymn, the preacher launched into a long rambling prayer for those brothers and sisters who lay on beds of affliction, and for those who had passed on and entered upon their everlasting rest, and were safely gathered in the arms of the great Redeemer. Keir was glad when it came to an end and they stood for another hymn.

The words of the prayers and hymns always puzzled Keir. They didn't make much sense to him. He sank into a day-dream, and followed the service mechanically until the preacher began his sermon.

'My dear brethren in Christ,' he said, 'my text is taken from the gospel according to St John, Chapter 8, verses 4 to 7.

'*They say unto him, Master this woman was taken in adultery, in the very act.*

Now Moses in the Law commanded us that such should be stoned, but what sayest thou?

This they said, tempting him, that they might have to accuse him.

'*When they continued asking him, he lifted up himself and said unto them, He that is without sin among you, let him cast the first stone.*'

Keir had hardly bothered to look at the preacher but when he heard the words about throwing a stone he looked up anxiously, and it seemed to him that as the preacher spoke he leant down and looked straight into his eyes—just as Major Goldie had looked at him when he had stood poised with the stone in his hand on the side of the cutting. He shrank back in the cold pew but the searching glance of the preacher seemed to seek him out. It wasn't possible that this man had seen him taking part in the riot. He came from another colliery. Why was he looking so deliberately at him? Was he going to denounce him as a scribe and a Pharisee, no better than one of the men who had stoned Stephen to death? If he had been able to get up and go out he would have done so, but he did not dare. Wouldn't that bring him even more clearly to the notice of the preacher? He shrank back in the pew, and prepared to be denounced.

No denunciation came, but Keir was glad when the sermon was over. As they came out after the last hymn he saw the preacher standing in the porch, shaking hands as he always did with the congregation as they left the chapel. He sidled past him, almost expecting to be called back and called to account. But nothing happened.

Many of the Hassop people went for a walk on Sunday after church, but Keir's mother had told him that some of her friends were coming for supper. He didn't want to go and listen to their gossip, and he knew that supper wouldn't be ready till nearly closing time or maybe after, when his father would bring his friends back with him. So he asked Jimmy if he would walk to Eshaw with him.

Eshaw was about three miles from Hassop. It was a small colliery in a valley on the far side of Hassop Hill, and connected with Durham by a railway that went in a loop around the hill. The few grammar school boys who lived there and at Cornhope farther on up the valley came to school by train, and these were the boys for whom the strike meant an unexpected holiday. Neither trains nor buses were running, and nobody expected them to walk the five or six miles to school and back every day.

Benny Darvell was one of the 'train boys' and he was in Keir's form. Keir liked him because he wasn't a swot or a creep. He had funny ear lobes that had no sensation in them. You could nip and even bite them and he would feel nothing. Keir knew that he would find him playing down by the burn or in the woods.

The two boys walked up past the allotments and the Aged

Miners' Homes and the old church of Bollington. There was a funny tombstone there, over the grave of two children who had been murdered a long time ago by a farm-servant. The inscription on the tombstone said, 'Here lie the bodies of Thomas and Martha Danby who were murdered by Robert Hinde who was duly hanged for his abominable crime.' But somebody had scratched out the name of the murderer till it could hardly be seen. Everybody said it was his father who was ashamed of him and wanted to blot out his name, so that he came every day and rubbed it with his stick; but he had died before he could completely erase the name.

It was a lovely evening. The larks were singing above the undrained fields fringed with rushes, and on the top of the hill peewits were wheeling and squirling. They passed the silent gray farm called Standalone, and dropped down into the Eshaw woods. As soon as they got into them Keir smelt the sharp peppery smell they always gave off, and heard Ben's voice calling through the undergrowth. At nesting time Ben spent all his free time in the wood or down by the beck.

'Wotchay, Keir. Are you still gannen to school?'

'Yes. We're not lucky like you. What's it like not having to go to school?'

'It's great. No lesson, no homework. What does Pa say about us not turnin' up?'

'He doesn't say anything. Some of the teachers still come late.'

'Is it true that Goldie's left?'

'He's not at school. He's blacklegging. He's driving a train. I saw him yesterday.'

'Is it true he's goin' to get the sack?'

'What for?'

'For stopping away. My dad says he hasn't got permission to stay off. He'll get his notice but he doesn't care, because he doesn't want to come back.'

'Is that true?'

'That's what my da says. He says he'll nivver come back.'

'I hope he doesn't. I nearly hit him with a brick yesterday.'

'Hey, did you hear that? Keir chucked a brick at Major Goldie and hit him.'

'I didn't exactly . . .' began Keir, but Ben didn't listen to him, and began shouting to all the others that Keir had hit the Major with a brick. They all started laughing and Keir didn't explain that far from hitting the Major he hadn't even thrown the stone, and had only been caught with one in his hand.

It didn't matter now. If Major Goldie was leaving the school he wouldn't be there when the strike ended to pick on him and punish him; and he wouldn't be there to tell Pa Walcott about him. A great weight was lifted off his mind. As they walked back over the hill it seemed to him that he was walking on the top of the world and there was nothing he was afraid of or anxious about.

As they walked back the two boys talked. Jimmy kept looking up admiringly at Keir as if he was a hero. Keir hated flattery, but he was glad of Jimmy's company, and they walked on happily together.

SEVEN

The Seventh Day

'Is the strike still on, da?' asked Keir. He was waiting for his mother to put his sandwiches in his school bag.

'It certainly is.'

'When is it going to finish?'

'When that Prime Minister of ours, Stanley Baldwin, sees sense and guarantees the men a decent living wage.'

'Will it be a long strike?'

'Why, the men winna give in, bonny lad. We're ganna stick it out to the finish, this time.'

Keir was relieved. As long as the strike was on he had nothing to fear from Major Goldie.

When he got to school somebody told him that there was a train running now from Eshaw, but the driver was a blackleg, and the miners wouldn't let their boys travel as long as he was on the footplate. So there were still no train boys. There were empty desks in every classroom, and History was almost a forgotten subject.

There was a shortage of prefects and it was still easy to sneak out of school and back in during the dinner break. It was too good a chance to miss, and Keir and Harry didn't mean to let it go begging.

As soon as they got into the market place they knew that

something was afoot. All along Silver Street the shopkeepers and their assistants were at the doors. And it seemed as if they were not there out of curiosity, but in readiness to defend their premises. The Black Maria that had carried off the man who tried to speak from the steps of the statue was back, parked near Doggarts; and near the statue there were four or five mounted policemen. It was strange to see the cold, lifeless statue of the horse and horseman on the plinth, and the living horses, standing almost as still and patient as the statue, grouped around it.

A bus approached the opening at the top of Silver Street. There was a civilian at the wheel, a policeman with him and barbed wire coiled over the bonnet. The policeman on duty at the top of the street put up his hand and stopped the bus, and Keir first heard and then saw a procession of men coming up the narrow street. At the head of the procession were three or four banners, not the big painted banners that the men carried on Big Meeting Day, but homemade affairs, old sheets tied to big bamboo canes, with slogans painted in red on them

'*Whose side are you on, Bishop?*'
'*What about Christian Charity now?*'
'*A new parable—Blessed are the Bosses.*'

There was no band, and the procession was not a large one. The men swung round at the top of Silver Street and into Saddler Street. They were clearly moving towards the cathedral. As they climbed Saddler Street and came to the Palace Green, the mounted police followed them; and Keir and Harry followed the police.

When they came to Palace Green they saw more mounted police drawn up in a long line in front of the cathedral and blocking the path leading down to the cathedral door. Like water blocked by an unexpected barrier the procession came to a halt and fanned out, some of the men moving on to the grass square in the middle of the Palace Green. Here the demonstrators and the police faced each other in complete silence. The only sounds to be heard were the clopping of the horses' hooves on the metalled roadway, the ruffling of the thin white banners, and the cathedral bells striking the quarters.

Then in silence Keir saw the door of the big cathedral open and from it came a clerical figure, dressed in black gaiters with a shovel hat in his hand, and after him came three or four priests, attired as if they had just been taking part in a service. The man in the gaiters seemed to be smiling as he came through the little opening in the sanctuary door, but the smile left his face as he saw, beyond the line of the policemen, the grim faces of the men and the threatening messages on their banners. He turned and retreated through the door, like one of those wrong-doers who used to come and take sanctuary in the cathedral; and as he turned and retreated a sullen murmur came from the men. There was a leaning forward of the banners, and a slow pressing forward of bodies—not a charge, not a riot but a kind of warning of rage barely suppressed. One of the policemen looked over his shoulder and said something that Keir couldn't catch. Then he must have touched his horse with his heel, because it tossed its head and lifted its two forefeet off the ground in a kind of dance, and then moved forward. A second and third moved forward, and Keir saw the whole body of mounted constables advance, some of them drawing their truncheons as they came. The men backed away and their banners began to jerk up and down like puppets. Then they turned and ran or were pushed back by the horses. One group broke and came running towards Keir and Harry. 'Down here!' said Harry, turning and running down one of the vennels that led into the Bailey. And when they had got out of sight and sound of the policemen, they flattened themselves against the wall and listened. They could hear the sound of horses cantering and feet running—but little else. No one cried out, there were no sounds of blows being given or taken. And when, a few minutes later, they ventured out on to the Green, all they could see were a few caps lying on the ground, a torn banner with broken poles, and two policemen standing over an old man who was lying half in the road and half in the gutter. Keir saw one of the policemen turn him over and say, 'Are ye all right, dad?' There was no sign of a blow or of blood on him. The rest of the men had fled down Saddler Street.

Then the cathedral bells rang again. They were late for school again. They didn't see what was happening in the market place because they took a short cut down Moatside Lane. There was no one on guard at the entrance to the school, but lessons had started. They hid in the lavatories till they heard the bell for the end of the first lesson. But before they could get to their seats, they heard Mr Smelley summoning them to come to his desk.

'Where have you two been?'

'Nowhere, sir.'

'Don't be such a fool, boy. Nobody can be nowhere. Where have you been? Why were you not here for the first lesson?'

There was nothing they could say.

'I see. You've been skipping lessons, eh? Taking French leave, eh? All right. Who's got the detention sheet? In go the names of our own little bolshie, Keir Ramsay, and his ever-faithful fellow-traveller, Henry Needham. That's the second in succession for you, isn't it, Ramsay?'

'Yes, sir.'

'One more time, my lad, and Mr Walcott will want to have a word with you.'

In detention that afternoon Pa Walcott came in as he often did and looked round at the offenders for the day. Keir thought that his eyes lingered a little longer than usual when they looked at him. But he said nothing, and went out. Keir settled down once more to the wearisome business of waiting for the fingers of the snail-like clock to move to half-past the hour.

EIGHT

The Eighth Day

Now that Keir was within one of a hat-trick of detentions—and three in a row meant being called up by the Head—for the first time since the strike had started, he began to consider he had better think twice before doing anything rash. Certainly he didn't dare risk another illicit visit to the city. So, though Harry would have risked it, Keir cried off.

But his caution turned out to be in vain. Just before afternoon-school began Neil Clough was showing everybody a stink bomb he had got hold of somewhere. Keir had never seen a stink bomb before and he asked him if he would let him touch it. Then just as it was being passed to him two other boys, Alan Marchant and Willy Lees, started fighting. 'Hey, be careful!' shouted Keir, but they either didn't hear him or didn't take any notice. They barged against Keir, then one of them tripped over the leg of a desk and fell heavily against him. The stink bomb jumped out of his hand and burst on the floor.

Immediately a horrible stench began to spread through the classroom—a mixture of rotten eggs, sulphuric acid, pig dung and sick. Keir, who couldn't stand bad smells, was on the point of vomiting, but he had to do something. He tried to scrape up the remains of the bomb on a piece of cardboard but he could hardly bear to go near it.

'Pooh, what a stink! Oh God, Keir, it's worse than your sweaty feet! Open the windows!'

All the boys who could bear to stay in the classroom took off their jackets and flapped them up and down, but the hateful smell would not be driven out. It seemed to cling to everything like an invisible fog, invading nose and mouth and throat.

'Watch out,' shouted somebody coming in from the corridor.

'It's Wright coming!'

Mr Wright could be heard coming with his jaunty step down the corridor, but as soon as he opened the classroom door he sniffed once, blew the air out of his lungs, then gave a long puff of disgust. Out came his hankie and a hand pressed it on his nose.

'Heavens above, what a disgusting stink! For goodness sake get away from those windows and let the fresh air come in. Take off your jackets, boys, and flap them about . . . No need to act the fool now! No need to flap around like old hens! . . . And leave that door open!'

It really was an appalling stench, so appalling that all the boys could do was to make funny faces and burst out laughing at one another as they flapped their jackets up and down. But Mr Wright was not amused. As soon as he could take his hankie from his nose, he said, 'Come on, now. Who was it? Who was responsible? Who made that stink? Whoever it was had better own up or else the whole class will be in detention tonight. Don't waste my time. Own up.'

After a few minutes Keir put his hand up.

'I dropped the . . . I dropped it, sir.'

'I might have known, mightn't I? If anybody gets up to mischief in this class you haven't to look far for the culprit, have you? Fetch me the detention sheet.'

'It was an accident, sir,' said Keir. 'It was knocked out of my hand.'

'Ah yes, I've heard that story before. Just an accident, sir. You have to pay for these little accidents.'

'Keir is right, sir,' said Alan Marchant. 'We were fooling on, sir and we bumped into him.'

'Who's we?'

'Me and Alan, sir,' said Willy Lees.

'Well, that's three of you to go down,' said Mr Wright. 'Ramsay and Lees and Marchant. Anybody else involved in this little affair?'

Nobody else spoke, not even the boy who had brought the stink bomb to school. Never mind, thought Keir, I'll give him a clout across the earhole when I get him to myself, but when he thought it over he decided to do nothing. It wasn't the boy's fault that it had been knocked out of Keir's hand; and he had better save his energies and wits to get himself out of trouble. The dreaded hat-trick of detentions had happened to him. He would have to face some stiff music now.

Mr Cohen, the French master, was on detention duty this time. He went through the roll, and then came back to Keir's name.

'Ramsay. Three detentions in a row. You know what that means, don't you?'

'Yes, sir.'

'The Headmaster will be sending for you, my boy, and I hope you say your prayers before you go to see him. All right. All of you sit still and make no noise for the next half-hour.'

After a few minutes they heard Mr Frogmore's gig coming up the street, heard a door slam and the noise of the pony clip-clopping away. Then the door opened and the Headmaster came in. He often came in like this, to hold a kind of review, and see how many malefactors there were. He walked round and didn't say anything till he came to Keir.

'Hum, haven't I seen you here before? Was it yesterday?'

'Yes, sir.'

'And now you've been misbehaving again, eh?'

'Yes, sir.'

'It seems to me that you'd better start mending your ways, young man, hadn't you?'

'Yes, sir.'

'Or else something very unpleasant is going to happen to you.'

Keir thought that Mr Cohen was going to tell the Head that this was his third detention; but he didn't. He simply remained standing till Pa had gone out, and then went back to his marking.

But he soon gave it up and, turning his back on the class, began to write something in tiny letters or figures on the blackboard. He was always doing this, and you couldn't see exactly what he was writing because he kept his body between the class and the board, and when he was finished he would clean the board so thoroughly that nobody could make out the marks. Some of the boys said he was a money-lender as well as a teacher, and he was reckoning up how much people owed him and what his interest would be. Whatever it was he was doing, it took him a long time. He was still writing on the blackboard when the cathedral bell struck the half-hour and he dismissed them.

As Keir was hurrying home he saw a man putting up a poster at a corner.

'*Strike Crisis Deepens*
Archbishop to Appeal to Nation Tonight'

But he wondered less what the Archbishop would say, than what he himself would say whenever the dreaded summons came to go to Pa Walcott's study.

NINE

The Ninth Day

Something important was clearly happening. After prayers a sixth-former came in to keep an eye on the class till the teacher arrived. All the teachers had been seen going into the Head's study. For a moment Keir thought they might all be discussing him, and wondering what to do with him; but when Mr Howard came in a few minutes later he said nothing unusual, but set them all to work repeating a conjugation they had just learnt as if nothing out of the ordinary had happened. But at the change-over of lessons the masters were seen talking together in small groups in the corridors. Then when the first lesson of the afternoon started they were all summoned to the Assembly Hall and the Head told them that the strike had ended at one o'clock that day.

'We have overlooked a great number of unusual practices,' he said, 'and turned a blind eye to many offences because I have been aware that the country has been passing through abnormal times. But the motto for everybody now is—back to normal. For the country and the school. We have a great deal of lost ground to make up, and I mean to see that you do it. All right. Now go back to your class-rooms quietly.'

So that was the end of the unexpected holiday for the train boys. The trains would be running tomorrow. But who had given in? His father had said that the men would never give in. Perhaps Mr Baldwin had given in or the Archbishop had given in. And what would happen to Major Goldie now? If the Major turned up and told Pa what Keir had been doing that Saturday afternoon just when Pa was looking at the detention reports and saw his name in red ink there—what would happen then?

His father was not in when he came home, and he and his mother had their tea without him. Mrs Ramsay said he had gone off on union business. The calling off of the strike had taken them all by surprise. She didn't say much. She was silent and worried.

When Keir went to bed his father had still not come home. Even when he heard his mother go to her bedroom his father had still not come in. Keir left the door of his bedroom open so that he would know when his father came, but he must have fallen asleep. When he woke he saw that the light was still on in the kitchen. His father must be still up.

Usually when his father stayed up he sat in the rocking chair and you could hear the springs creaking. But this time there was no sound. Keir went to the foot of the stairs to see if there was anything the matter with him. His father was sitting in the chair quite still. Keir couldn't be sure whether he was asleep or not. The light from the electric bulb in the middle of the room fell on his brow and the side of his cheek. He had not bothered to stir the fire. The ashes had fallen revealing one dull red hollow, but the rest was cold and gray.

Keir didn't say anything to him, but went back to bed and shut his door as quietly as he could.

The next day the train boys were all back at school. The Head told them in 'Assem' that he wanted to see them all in the detention room—the Physics Lab.—as soon as the registers had been called. When Mr Smelley had filled in the register he asked all those boys who had been absent during the strike to put their hands up.

'All right. You all have to go to the Physics Lab to see the Headmaster. And I hope he makes it hot for you. . . . And talking about making it hot etc., I think there's somebody else that's in for a wigging. Yes—that's you, Ramsay. So you'd better go along as well.'

They hadn't long to wait before the Head came in. He mounted the rostrum and for some reason turned the water on in the tap that stood over the demonstration sink, let it run for a second and then turned it off.

'I understand from your form masters,' he said, 'that you boys did not come to school last week. Is that true?'

'Yes, sir.' It was a mumbled reply; and at the end of it Keir said clearly, 'No, sir.'

'Why did you say no, boy, when all the rest said yes?'

'I'm not a train boy, sir, I've been sent to you for another reason.'

'Well you just stand aside over there and I'll deal with you later. The rest of you—what was the reason for your absenting yourselves?'

'No trains, sir. We're all train boys.'

'It was the General Strike, sir.'

'But there were trains. After the first few days a train came in from Eshaw and Scorburn every day. Why didn't you catch those trains. You, Simpson, you're a sixth former, aren't you? Why didn't you come on that train?'

'My father wouldn't let me, sir.'

'Why not?'

'He said the drivers were blacklegs, sir.'

'Did he? Well now let me tell you—and I want you to tell your fathers this—you are under a legal obligation to go to school every day. And what is more, your fathers and mothers are under a legal obligation to see that you get there. They have been breaking the law. And I want you to tell your parents that it is more than likely that they have not yet seen the end of this affair. People who break the law must expect to be punished. But since you were acting in obedience to your legal guardians, I do not propose to punish you. But let me say this. The strike is over. You have lost some ground in the last nine days and I expect you to make it up. You can go now . . . Now (turning to Keir) you, boy, I remember you now. Three days running you were in detention, weren't you?'

'Yes, sir.'

'What were you up to?'

'I did the wrong homework, sir. I went into the city without permission, and I dropped a stink bomb—by accident, sir.'

'A nice record, isn't it? While the country has been brought to the brink of civil war, while every decent man in the country has been trying his hardest to bring this disastrous affair to a close—what have you been doing? Playing the fool, neglecting instructions, taking French leave and then this last stupid prank. You are a stupid boy, Keir Ramsay. And you're all the more stupid because you have some brains. You needn't look up at me like that. You're wondering, aren't you, that a boy can be intelligent and stupid at the same time. Well you can, and you are. You could do well for yourself. Mr Howard has told me that. You could have a good career ahead of you. But I'm going to tell you plainly that if you don't stop playing the fool, I'll expel you. I'll kick you out of this school and I'll see to it that you never get back into it. And that will be the end of your career—for good. And what will your father think of that? And what will you think when you have to change your school uniform for a miner's clothes and go down the pit—that is, if anybody will be kind enough to take you on. This school can be a golden gate for you, my boy, but as sure as fate, if you don't stop playing the fool, I'll lock that gate behind you and you'll never get through it again. Off you go. No, caning won't do you any good. Off you go—and tell your father what I've said to you—if you dare.'

Keir did not say anything to his father of what the Head had said to him. But he had never been spoken to so earnestly and impressively. It was the turning-point of his life.

PART THREE

Aftermath

ONE

Alone

The Great Strike was over, but not for Keir's father or his workmates or any of the men who worked in the coal-mines of Britain. The railwaymen, the bus-drivers, the electricians, the shipyard workers all went back to work; but for the miners nothing had been won. They were left with nothing but the harsh terms that had been put to them before the strike. They felt that they had been betrayed; but, although they knew that they were now on their own they still would not accept the wage cuts the owners wished to force on them. The owners, for their part, were more than ever determined to starve the men into submission. They had won the first round, and felt confident they could win the second.

For Keir's father the failure of the strike was a bitter blow. 'But we're not beaten yet!' he said. 'We've been let down shamefully—aye, by the very folk that should ha' stood by us. But by God we're not finished yet. Not by a lang chalk!'

For Keir, too, the days of the strike had been humiliating. The solemn warning that the Headmaster had given him had made him at last see how close he was to disgrace. The gates of the pit were locked against his father. Now, if he didn't mend his ways, the gates of the school and all that that meant would be locked against him. And he had enough sense to realise that though his father had been the victim of others, the shame that hung over him was the consequence of his own stupidity.

In those few days Keir began to grow up. If his father could face his fate with courage, he too would seek the strength of mind to mend his ways. Ever since he had gone to the Grammar School he had played the fool and put his energy into stupid courses. Now he would put it to better ends. The prospect of having to come home one day and say to his father, 'I'm a failure. They've expelled me,' was one that filled him with shame. His father and mother had already been let down by those who ought to have befriended them. He did not mean to join the ranks of their betrayers.

From then on a change came over him. So far he had done little to make his parents proud of him, in spite of all they had done for him; but out of the wreck of the family fortunes there was still something to be saved and he meant to save it.

One thing helped him—Major Goldie never returned to school. Some said that he had been hauled over the coals for staying away during the strike, and the Governors had forced him to resign; but Keir's father said he had gone to be agent for a Tory candidate in a constituency in Yorkshire, and what he was really after was being a Conservative candidate himself. Whatever the explanation, he never came back, and his place was taken by a young man who didn't believe in Warner and Martin and was a far better teacher. So no one ever told Pa Walcott how Keir had joined the rioters on that fateful Saturday, and there was one less offence for him to have to explain away.

All through that summer the coal-miners' strike dragged on. Only the safety men went down the pit, and day after day, week after week, not a single tub of coal came to the surface. The customary supply of free coal was cut off. Fortunately the weather was fine and mild, but no miner's wife could do without a fire. There was cooking and baking to do and water had to be heated for the weekly wash. The men had to find their own supplies of fuel in the big spoil heaps that lay around the pithead. The men dug into these, until the heaps were scarred with craters like shell-holes, and picked out, piece by piece, the precious small coal, filling old sacks and wheeling them or carrying them home on their backs. The men liked the work. It gave them something to do and it kept them from going soft. They had spent all their lives digging and shovelling and shifting heavy loads and idleness was bad for them. They scoured the countryside looking for the best slagheaps, and sometimes spent all day there, happy to be doing a shift of work again, eating their bait there as they would have done if they had been at work. They were born workers, and hated being idle.

But money grew shorter and shorter. The Friday luxuries that Keir had once looked forward to—a packet of custard cream biscuits or fig rolls—disappeared. Once they had all had bacon and egg for breakfast, but now there was nothing but a salty little half-rasher. Fortunately vegetables were plentiful and cheap. At least once a week Keir's mother made an immense pan of thick broth, with a little ham-bone in it, and they'd have this for at least two days. But they had little fruit. Keir's teeth, which had never been good, began to decay faster, and he suffered agonies from toothache. The school dentist sent him off to the clinic at Chester-le-Street, but he went only once: his mother couldn't afford the bus-fare.

There was just enough to live on, but not enough to replace anything that broke or wore out. Keir heard his mother talking one day about a big family in the next street where they drank their tea out of jam jars. Most of the men had to do their own cobbling and instead of leather they used the rubber from old car-tyres. Some children had no shoes at all, and didn't go to school. Some of the men collected coltsfoot leaves, dried them and put them in their pipes instead of tobacco.

It wasn't only the miners who suffered. The shopkeepers who depended on them also began to face hard times. One day when Keir was walking across the square he saw Mr Futers standing in the doorway of his shop. His was one of the few shops still open. Many of the others had closed down and big notices in black letters 'TO LET' were stuck diagonally across the empty windows. Some of the shops were boarded up to stop boys from breaking the windows. Mr Futers still kept his brother on, though he did poor business now, but he had sacked the old man who had worked for him for years, and was running the business single-handed. He looked pale and overworked and anxious. Keir saw nobody going into the shop. The windows were pasted over with home made signs 'BARGAINS GALORE'—'GREAT REDUCTIONS'—'TEN PER CENT OFF SHIRTS AND TROUSERS'—but under these was another notice, less welcoming,

'NO CREDIT GIVEN'

Keir gave him a wide berth. He had been to see Chas only once since that night when Mr Futers had misled him about the geometry problems—and on that occasion Mr Futers had lost his temper and abused Mr Ramsay and all the other men at the Bishop who were ruining the country with their obstinate strikes and driving honest hard-working shopkeepers out of business. Keir had never gone to Poverty Street since that day. He didn't want to speak to Mr Futers. He hated him.

Week after week it grew more difficult to make ends meet. Buying new clothes was out of the question for most families in the colliery. Even 'poor Cyril', as he was still called, had to give up calling with his cases of cheap blouses and shirts and packets of pins; and as soon as his brother found that there was no profit to be made out of him, Cyril was given to understand that he couldn't be kept on any longer. They said that he had gone south, to Leicester or Coventry, but the truth was that nobody knew what had become of him. The Friday market was still held, but now there were more second-hand clothes stalls than anything else. Mrs Ramsay couldn't bring herself to buy other people's cast-offs. Instead she darned and mended and patched, turning dresses and skirts, and cutting up whatever was past patching or mending for clippings for her mats.

Food was scarce, but sometimes the fishman would appear with a cart-load of caller-herring and sell them off at a penny each; and every week Mrs Ramsay went to help Mrs Jamieson, who kept pigs, and made meat-pies to sell cheaply to the women of the colliery. Thanks to Mrs Jamieson there were pies at least once a week, and from time to time black puddings and even a leg of pork.

But the Co-op order got smaller and smaller every week, and people began to sell off their insurance for pitiful sums. They said that the foxy-faced little insurance man was making a nice packet buying them up for himself. But people were only too glad to have a little ready money, and didn't ask too many questions.

Fortunately it was summer, and the men found it easy to mine enough small coal from the slagheaps to keep going. The boys picked bilberries and blackberries. They chewed the little green hawthorn shoots called 'bread and cheese', dug up 'arnicks', and even ate the soft mushy haws when they ripened.

The men found it hard to fill their days. They walked through the fields, waving little hawthorn switches over their heads to keep off the flies, played quoits and handball and endless games of cards and dominoes. Some of them took refuge in the sheds they had built on their allotments. Their wives didn't want them at home and they were glad to 'hole in' anywhere. Some of the younger men, despairing of ever getting back to work, tried to enlist, but many of them came back from the medical tribunal crestfallen. They had been turned down because they were not fit enough.

But they all lived on in hopes that sooner or later the owners would give in. They never dreamt seriously of seeking work elsewhere. The colliery was their life. They hadn't the heart or the energy to leave and seek a new life among strangers.

Some of the young people, desperate for fun, began to group themselves into jazz bands and parade up and down, beating tambourines and blowing on their submarines. Collieries began organising carnivals in which the bands competed against one another. But Keir never joined them. He was beginning to have other things on his mind.

TWO

A New World

At the beginning of the summer holidays Mrs Ramsay had a letter from her sister Linda. Linda lived in Cumberland and was married to Thomas Atkinson, the hero of one of the many family stories Keir's mother had told him from time to time. Linda had been engaged to Henry Green, a young butcher who worked in the covered market at Newcastle, but she went into service near Keswick, met a young farm labourer and threw Henry over. There had been a famous scene when Henry had gone over to Keswick to have things out with Linda and had been punched on the nose by Thomas and nearly pitched into the lake at Bassenthwaite. Thomas was one of Keir's heroes, although he had only seen him once or twice in his life.

In her letter Linda sent Keir's train fare to Bassenthwaite and said that she would take him off Lizzie's hands for two weeks. That would mean one less to feed, and maybe by the time he came home the strike would be settled.

So, a few days after they had joyfully sung in 'Assem'

Lord, dismiss us with thy blessing

Keir began on the second longest journey of his life, and towards the end of the day, having changed trains at Barnard Castle, Kirkby Stephen, and Penrith, and having crossed the

Pennines—mountains that had before existed for him only in his atlas and his geography textbook—he found himself walking from the little station at Bassenthwaite with his Uncle Thomas.

The road was quiet and dusty. To the right, through the trees, glimmered the immense still lake, the surface broken only where a fish rose and spread a glittering ring of ripples; and beyond the lake the great rounded mountain of Skiddaw. The sound of somebody talking at the far side of the lake came clearly over the still water. Before they came to Crakehouse Cottage they passed a little jetty running out into the lake.

'Is that where Henry threw the ring into the water?' asked Keir.

'Wheer hes t' heerd that tale?'

'My mother told me.'

'That's t'spot a'reet. He com ower 'ere an' started roonnen' yer aunt down, so a banged him, reet on t'end of 'is nose. 'E was joost a laal feller an' 'e didn't tek mooch knockin' down. And then he roon out to t' end o' that jetty theer, an' 'e took t' ring out of 'is pocket—she'd sent it back to 'im—an' 'e choocked it reet out in t'watter.'

'Did you ever find it?'

'A nivver looked. As far as a knaw, it's still theer. Ya thing's for sure, 'e nivver coom back efter that clout I gi' 'im.'

Crakehouse Cottage was at the far end of the lake. It was bigger than the house Keir lived in in Brunel Street, with a big yard at the back with a closet, a woodshed and a big pigsty with three porkers in it that Thomas was fattening, and a big garden full of vegetables. Beyond the yard was a field and at the bottom of the field a copse where Thomas gathered what he called 'kin'lin'' and where there were so many young rabbits you could run them down. There was no electricity in the cottage, but that didn't make much difference because they had oil lamps, and in any case nobody stayed up once the darkness came down.

On the first Sunday he was there his uncle took him out fishing. He hadn't a proper rod, but he cut one from a hazel tree, and Thomas gave him a length of line and a few hooks and showed him where to get worms. The first expedition was disastrous. Keir let his fish off the hook and in addition kicked the tin of worms over into the water. To his surprise Thomas wouldn't fish any more from there.

'We might as weel pack oop,' he said. 'We'll nivver git anoother bite 'ere.'

'Why not?'

'Yon fish thoo let off, it'll a' gone straight back te a' t'oothers in t'watter, an' tellt them there's a coople o' fellers fishin' off t' jetty theer. So thoo'll nivver git anoother bite, noot frae 'ere.'

But he allowed Keir to start fishing again from another point. They caught nothing but bass, which Thomas said nobody would eat, except the cat; but they were the first fish that Keir had ever caught. There were no fish in the river that ran past Eshaw. It was too dirty.

Sometimes his uncle took him to work with him and he helped him to scythe down nettles in the pastures, dig out ditches, get the cows in for milking or mend gates. One day he went out blackberrying and collected so many that his aunt said they should take them to Keswick market. They got little more for them than would pay the train fare but they had a day out; and when they had sold their blackberries his aunt took him to see some of Thomas's relations who gave him rum butter for tea and laughed at him when he was eating it.

Best of all was the swimming. Day after day he went down to the jetty and dived in from the end. He had never swum in the open air before. He had learnt to swim and dive in the baths at Durham, but there was nowhere to swim at Hassop. Here there was a whole lake of clear water, and a diving board in the form of a jetty. Day after day he plunged in, swimming out to where he thought the ring might have fallen, diving and pressing his face against the bottom of the lake to look for it. He never found it, but in searching he found something else.

When he got back to Hassop his mother looked at him in surprise.

'Ye look a different lad. Here, look at this, Davy, he's put on pounds. If he goes on like this all his clothes will need altering.'

In a fortnight he seemed to have grown inches. He had filled out, and his skin was brown with the sunshine and fresh air. Chopping wood, chasing rabbits, climbing the slopes of Skiddaw, swimming in the lake, scything down nettles—all this exercise had hardened him and given him colour and strength. Beside him his father looked pale and thin.

THREE

The Cundy Again

In the middle of September the new school year began. Once more, heavily and reluctantly, the whole school went through the customary hymn

Lord, behold us with thy blessing

Keir was a fifth-former now. At the end of the year he would be taking School Certificate, and after that the Head would decide if he was good enough to go into the Sixth. In the meanwhile new set books were given out—Julius Caesar, Eothen and The Lay of the Last Minstrel. . . .

But the men at Hassop, at Eshaw, and Lemside, were still all on strike. Neither side had given in. The great strike of last May was only a memory now. The miners had been on their own for nearly five months—more than five months—and summer was ending. A mood of despair was beginning at last to settle on the men. Idleness, bad food, poverty, frustration and humiliation were all beginning to take their toll.

One night when Keir was sitting doing his homework in his favourite corner, the door opened and a tall long-jawed man in a cap and muffler came in and stood in the doorway.

Keir and his mother both looked up. She was up to her elbows in flour. It was Tommy Blenkinsop who had once worked marras with Mr Ramsay. They had broken up some time ago, but there had been no quarrel. The two men were still friends.

'Is Davy not in then?' he asked.

'He's at a lodge meeting.'

The man hesitated, looking round the room in a bold, impolite way. Then, as if he had seen enough, he said, 'I expect I'll catch him there,' and went out, shutting the door noisily.

'Well I must say he had a good look, didn' he?' said Mrs Ramsay. 'He should recognise this place the next time he sees it.'

She didn't like Tommy Blenkinsop. He was a good-looking man in a bold kind of way, and one of the best workers in the Bishop. Keir had often heard his father talk about him. He would take nothing to the pit for his 'bait' but a pit-bottle of cold tea, work like a demon from the beginning to the end of the shift, then go home and eat a huge meal.

'Lad, I've nivver seen anybody shift the amount that he can when he comes in from work. He eats as much as three men. But he's a good worker. I must give him credit for that.'

But Mrs Ramsay didn't trust him. Everybody knew he was a bad husband, and his plain little wife had a thin time with him. He had never shown her his paynote in all the years of their married life.

'No, I dinna trust him,' said Mrs Ramsay. 'He's a bad 'un. He'll be up to summat shady, I bet. And I hope your da has mair sense than get mixed up wi' him.'

The next night Tommy paid a second visit. He didn't knock, but pushed open the door and came in when he saw his old marra sitting in the rocking chair. Mrs Ramsay wasn't in. It was the night on which she helped Mrs Jamieson.

'Hes tha got a few minutes, Davy?'

'Aye. Come in. Sit thysel down.'

'I was just thinkin', Davy, we might dee oursels a bit of

good in the next few days.'

'How's that?'

'There's three trucks of good coal standing in the sidings.'

'Have they got anybody keeping an eye on them?'

'They have a feller there during the day, but I think he knocks off when it gets dark. I dinna see why we shouldn't help oursels to a few bags if we set about it the right way. They're supposed to be for the manager, but it might be a few days afore they start carting them up to his place.'

'What's in thy mind then, Tommy?'

'If we wait till after twelve we should be able to snaffle a few bags. They'll nivver be missed.'

'Why, I must say that we could do wi' a bit of good coal. It's poor stuff that I got last time from the Heap.'

'I'll tell tha what. I'll come round just after twelve toneet. Put thy pit claes on and black thy face and naebody will ivver see us.'

Keir's father never kept anything secret from his wife—or from Keir. He told Mrs Ramsay what he was going to do, and told Keir to stay up to give him a hand to get the coal into the coalhouse as soon as they came back. Mrs Ramsay tried to persuade him to give up the idea.

'For heaven's sake, dinna get mixed up with that Tommy Blenkinsop,' she said. 'If ye get a summons the Lord knows who'll pay for it. It's bad enough feeding the pair of you.'

After she had gone to bed Keir sat up watching his father making his preparations. He put on his pit clothes and the little slush cap he wore when he was working in a wet seam; then as soon as he heard Tommy knocking on the door—this was the signal they had arranged on—he put his hand up the inside of the chimney, covered it with soot and blackened his face with it.

Keir turned to his book but he couldn't keep his mind on what he was reading. He began to wonder what the two men were doing. Suddenly he was filled with a desire to join them, perhaps to stand guard for them. He knew where they would be. He put down his book, pulled on his jacket, and at the last minute blackened his own hands and face as his father had done. He hurried down to the siding and as he came close he could hear the scrape of a shovel and the sound of the coal falling into the sacks. He settled down to keep guard for them.

He was just in time. Someone else was crossing the lines, from time to time switching on a torch to look into the doorways of the smiths' shops and the dark corners of the colliery offices. Keir knew who it was. Only one man in the colliery had a torch with that powerful beam—P C Lightwood, the Hassop bobby. Someone had told him to keep an eye on the trucks and he was making for them now, stopping at every turn to shine his torch on any suspicious form or shape. Keir waited until he had turned away to look at something that had caught his notice then quickly went over to where his father was working.

'Da! Da! There's somebody coming. I think it's the bobby.'

'Lad, tha nearly frightened the wick out o' me coming up like that. What makes you think it's the bobby?'

'I've seen his torch. It's very strong. If he shines it on you he'll get your names and you'll get a summons.'

'We'd better get off as quick as we can,' said Tommy Blenkinsop.

'I can show you a good place to hide.'

'Haway then. We'll follow.'

He led them to the edge of the tip, and they all began to slither down it. It was impossible to move without making a noise. As they slid down the scree, sending loose stones rolling before them in an invisible avalanche, they heard a voice behind them calling on them to stop and give themselves up.

When they came to the bottom Keir said, 'Get into the cundy. Quick!'

'Nae good gannin in there,' said Tommy. 'We'll be trapped. Ye can only get in a few yards.'

'I know how to get past the grill,' said Keir. 'Come on. I'll show you.'

It was pitch black inside the tunnel, but Keir went boldly on till he felt the grating; then he quickly removed the loose bars.

'Squeeze through. And go on for a dozen yards or so. Go on. You won't fall into anything. It's wet but it's safe—just a trickle of water. Get well in and don't stir.'

They squeezed through the bars. Tommy was a well-built man and Keir heard something rip as he pushed through. As soon as both the men were through he put the bars back into place and guided the men till he had brought them, as far as he could judge, to the bend in the tunnel.

The night was so still that he could hear the policeman slither down the slope, reach the bottom and look round. He came over to the mouth of the cundy, and flashed his torch inside it. Keir knew that the beam had fallen on the grating because he could see the shadows of the bars on the wet wall of the tunnel. He held his breath, for five, for ten seconds. Then the light moved away, and he could hear the policeman blundering off, snapping the twigs of the dead buried trees as he stumbled against them. When that sound ceased he knew they were safe.

'He's gone, da.'

'Ye sure?'

'Yes, but I'll slip out first and make certain.'

He crept cautiously out of the cundy and looked round. He could see the beam of the bobby's torch playing on the twisted shapes of dead and dying trees, on the rusty sides of abandoned tubs, on drifts of dry willow herb.

'Is the coast clear, Keir?' asked Tommy.

'Yes. But I think you'd better give up the coal. They might

have somebody else watching.'

'Damn to one,' said Tommy, 'I'm not givin' that up now.'

'I'll keep a look-out for you.'

In half an hour they were safe at home, and had stowed the coal safely away in the coalhouse. Keir's mother never knew what part he had played in the night's escapade. All she knew was that for the next fortnight she had the best coal she had had for months. It was so good she almost forgave Tommy Blenkinsop, blackguard though she knew him to be.

But Keir's father could never be persuaded to repeat the raid.

'No,' he said. 'I dinna mind a fair fight, but I draw the line at pinching things. If I canna get what I want without breaking the law, I'll dee without it.'

What troubled him most, however, was not the realisation of how close he had been to being caught, but how near he had come to involving Keir in his disgrace.

FOUR

A Prize At Last

Keir had never made much of a mark as a scholar. He had never considered himself as one of the brightest in any of the forms in which he had been put. To tell the truth, he had never had any desire to shine, except at football, or fighting. His main desire had been to enjoy himself, not to get into too many scrapes, to occupy an inconspicuous position somewhere in the middle of the class, and to leave prizes to the brainy ones—Matty Pocock, Ralph Bell, and Alan Newton—who year after year were summoned to the Speech Day that he had never attended. He had never had the least desire to be like Matty, for instance, who came top of the form year after year. He had never looked upon himself as ever having the brains to emulate him.

But one day it came to him that if he tried he could rise in the form, and not even the brainy Matty Pocock was invincible.

Mr Howard had a test of his own called the 'Ring Test.' He would get the boys out of their desks and string them out in a long line at the front of the classroom. He would take up a position at the back of the classroom and begin to fire questions at them. If the first boy was stumped he passed on to the next and the next, and the first boy to give the correct answer moved up above those who had failed.

Keir had always liked this test. He liked almost everything that Mr Howard did, but this was more like a game than a lesson. He liked being challenged and being promoted instantly if he rose to the challenge.

He started low down in the order—the class was always set out in strict alphabetical order to begin with—and at first he made little headway. The questions seemed easy and were answered before they came to him. But suddenly he heard Mr Howard asking a question that the leaders didn't seem to be able to answer.

'What is Ultima Thule? And where is it? Two parts to this question and you have to get both parts.'

Nobody knew. One, two, three, four, five, six boys had the question put to them, but it stumped them all. How Keir knew that Ultima Thule was the Latin for the Orkneys and the Shetlands, he wasn't quite certain. He couldn't remember where he had picked it up. This was the kind of thing that happened so often in Mr Howard's lessons. It was a kind of telepathy.

There was still a dozen in front of Keir to be questioned and among them were Matty Pocock and Alan Newton. Ralph Bell had already failed. Now it was Matty's turn to fail, and Alan's turn to fail, and the question came to Keir. He gave the right answer, he moved at one step to the top of the column. Nobody that day had made such a jump and the class broke out into clapping.

He didn't stay there, but this moment of triumph, the first occasion on which he had publicly outshone Matty and Ralph and Alan and all the other boys whom he had thought far cleverer than he was, made him more determined than ever to prove to everybody that he wasn't the numskull they had all thought him. For the first time since he had shown what was in him by getting a place in the Grammar School, he felt keen to do well. There was more of his father in him than he suspected. He was a fighter and he had found something to fight for.

For the rest of the term he immersed himself in the world of school. He forgot the strike, the shortage of coal and food, shabby clothes, the rubber soles on his boots and the lumpy darns in the heels of his stockings. These things meant less to him than Wheatstone's Bridge, the analysis of salts, the Golden Treasury and Macaulay's History of England, quadratic equations, Caesar, French irregular verbs, the fourth book of Euclid and the geography of Africa and the French Revolution . . . He ceased to go with Pompey, and spent no more hours exploring the Cundy, teasing frogs, throwing stones at the pots on the top of telegraph posts. It wasn't that he loved all that he did. No, he had begun to feel his strength and he didn't want to be beaten—that was all there was to it. And as his work improved his teachers began to change towards him. Even Mr Smelley stopped teasing him about his name. He was no longer the bolshie boy with the bolshie name; and when the results came out at the end of the term he found he had been awarded a prize—the prize for the boy who had made the greatest advance during the year. Before this he had scorned prizes, but now he was glad that at last he would be able to go to a Speech Day, and his mother and father would be invited to see him get his prize.

FIVE

The Bishop

In September a new football season opened. A few men still found something to put on the coupons, but Mr Metcalf had given them up. Keir still went to see him from time to time, because he was a cheerful old man and always had something to make a joke about. Keir's own father was preoccupied with the strike and the coming surrender to the owners. He had taken to listening to the news on the crystal set—the only paper they took now was the Friday 'Durham Chronicle'—but most of what he heard disheartened him. Some miners in the Midlands had already given in and gone back to work. Only the men of South Wales, Yorkshire, Durham and Northumberland were left to carry on the struggle. Day by day he became less certain of victory, and more and more convinced that sooner or later he and his friends would have to give in.

But Mr Metcalf was more philosophical. 'Ah well,' he said, 'If we're beaten we've given them a good run for their money. And we weren't the first to show the white feather. We might get some good out of it in the lang run. Efter all work's work, and it's better than sitting all day on your backside. I'll be glad when I get on the footplate of my little tankie again.'

Mr Metcalf had never worked at the coal-face. He was a

colliery engine driver, driving the little shunting engines or 'tankies' as they were called, that were used to move the trucks in the colliery sidings. He once told Keir that he would have liked to be an engineer, but lack of schooling had held him back.

'Aye that's what's kept me where I am, Keir. The calculations—they're all beyond me. I nivver had a proper training. If I did I nivver took it in.'

He was a thoughtful old man and used to ask Keir how he was getting on at school.

'You tek ivvery chance you can, Keir. That's what I'm always saying to our Jimmy here. Ye nivver can tell but I might be talking to two future members of parliament, mightn't I? That would mek thy father and mother tek notice, wouldn' it?'

From time to time he would give Keir books to read—'The Earthly Paradise' by William Morris, and 'The Ragged Trousered Philanthropist'—but he didn't enjoy them as much as 'King Solomon's Mines' and 'Eric Brighteyes'.

One night he set out after he had finished his homework to take back to Mr Metcalf a book he had lent him. As soon as he got out into the street he knew that something unusual was afoot. The women were standing at their doors calling out to each other, and he saw Pompey come running down the street on his way to the square.

'What's up, Pompey?'

'The Bishop's here and the men are going to get him.'

'Which Bishop?'

'The Bishop of Durham, man. Which one do ye think?'

'What's he here for?'

'I divven' knaa. Are ye coming?'

Keir went back into the house and put the book back on the table, then ran down the street after Pompey. From what Pompey had told him he expected to see the square full of people, but it looked as empty as ever, with the pale street lights at the far side reflected in the damp tarmac like lamps in a black pool. But when he looked carefully he could see small groups of men and women standing in the shop openings and at the dark corners where the light from the street lamps did not fall. He saw Mrs Harrigan, one of his mother's neighbours, standing with her black shawl pulled round her, and he went over and asked her where the Bishop was.

'In there, hinny,' she said, pointing to the Rectory. 'They say there's been a confirmation or summat. He's inside there now with the parson. You would wonder how he dared come here after what he's said about us.'

The Bishop had never been on the side of the miners. He had made it plain over and over again that he didn't like the strike, and he'd gone so far as to tell a reporter from Newcastle that if the miners' wives would learn how to cook simple and wholesome meals instead of buying cheap biscuits and fish and chips they would find that the wages the men got were more than enough. The men disliked him, and what he had said in the interview infuriated them.

Keir and Pompey ran over to look at the big black car drawn up outside the Rectory. The chauffeur was in the driver's seat, with the inside light switched on, and they peered in at him like people peering at fish in a tank.

'What do you lads want?' he said, winding down the window.

'Nothing. We're just looking.'

'Then get yersels away. What's the matter with ye? Hev ye nivver seen a motor car afore? Go on, clear off!'

They went back to where Mrs Harrigan was, and stood watching the car, until the door of the Rectory opened and a man in a long dark cloak came out.

'That's him,' said Mrs Harrigan, and pushed past Keir. He could see other men and women making for the car, but the chauffeur had already started it. He swung it round and made a bee-line for the far corner of the square. As he accelerated men and women seemed to spring up from nowhere, and as the car turned to enter the Durham Road its headlights fell on a solid mass of men and women drawn up and blocking the road. It was impossible to break through such a barrier. The car came to a standstill. Keir saw the Bishop lean forward to speak to the chauffeur and the sunshine roof was pulled back so that the Bishop could stand up and see what was happening. He turned round slowly, looking steadily to the crowd, and listening without a trace of fear or concern to the storm of boos and catcalls that broke out all round him.

He put up his hand, and the booing died down. 'men,' he said, 'men—and women. I am pleased to have the opportunity to say a few words to you. I know why you are here. You don't like what I have said about your strike . . .'

The booing broke out again, but he waited until it subsided and went on.

'Well, I'm not going to say that I'm sorry. I'm not going to take back anything I said. You see, I'm not a politician.'

'Then tha should keep out of politics! And mind thy own business,' shouted someone from the back of the crowd.

'I repeat—I am not a politician. In my profession I have to tell the truth.'

'Aye—for the bosses!'

'Tha wants to tell the truth about the men for a change!'

'And the women!'

'I speak for no side,' said the Bishop. 'I speak for the Church—and I speak for myself.'

'Aye, you're well enough off!' shouted another woman, and the booing broke out again.

'Of course I am. I don't go on strike. But listen to me. And I'll pay you this compliment. You'll listen to me better if I'm straight with you than if I try to flatter you. Are the miners in this country any worse off than thousands of others in the land? I've worked among farm-labourers and I've worked in the East End of London. . . .'

'And what did you do to help them?'

'And it didn't stop tha from wearing a gold chain around thy neck!'

For the first time the Bishop looked surprised. He must have forgotten his gold chain. Keir hadn't noticed it either till the woman had mentioned it. Now he could see it clearly. He saw the Bishop's hand close over it as if, for a moment, he was afraid that someone might snatch it.

'This?' he said, holding it up.

'Aye—that cost plenty, I bet.'

'What about selling that and giving it to the poor?'

'Why should I? Why should I sell it? I'll tell you the story of this cross, and then you can judge for yourselves. Before I came here I worked in London. Have you ever seen the East End of London? Sometimes I hear you men grumbling, but I tell you, as a man of God, that this village, for all its slagheaps and its smoke, is Paradise compared with the East End. But I won't go into that. What I want to tell you is that I worked for years among those East-enders, and when I left the last thing the men and women did for me was to buy me this chain and cross. "Wear this for us," they said. "Wherever you are, keep this and wear it in remembrance of us." Now let me ask you all a straight question. Would you sell this if it had been given to you on those conditions? Would you sell a sacred keepsake that had been given to you by your friends? You needn't answer. I don't need an answer. I know you and I know that you would have done exactly what I have done.'

A silence had fallen on the crowd. Keir looked at the men and women around him. They looked puzzled, and tongue-tied. When the Bishop began to speak to them again they did not interrupt him. He thanked everybody for listening to him so patiently. Then he sat down, the chauffeur started the car, and the crowd parted before it as it edged forward.

As it drove away a few men on the edge of the crowd began to mutter but most of them drifted away into the darkness. Keir could see the red tail light of the Bishop's car diminishing and then vanishing, and the vague forms of the men and women melting into the darkness.

'Why did you let the Bishop go, da?' he asked his father.

'What could we dee, hinny? We stand up for our rights, but we dinna stain our hands wi' somebody else's blood. He's nae friend of ours, that feller, but he's a man, like the rest of us. And I'll tell tha summat else.'

'What?'

'He's clivver. Ower clivver for us. Man, we're just clay in the hands of men like that. Just clay.'

That night was the beginning of the end for the men of Durham and Northumberland. Late in November the Yorkshire miners decided that they could hold out no longer. Now the men of the North Country and the men of South Wales were alone. It was impossible for them to resist further. Early in December, the men of Durham and Northumberland, the last to hold out, accepted the coal owners' terms. They had held out for seven months, and had gained nothing.

SIX

New Friends

It was Friday night again. All the callers had come and gone, except Cyril. He had never returned to Hassop, and Mr Futers hadn't found anyone who would slave for him as his brother had done. Keir could hear the metal swinging of the scales as the last of the callers—the sanctimonious butcher—moved on along the street, his cart swaying and lurching in and out of the ruts.

Mr Ramsay was sitting in front of the fire reading the *Chronicle*. He was waiting for his marra. They always went to the Club together on Friday nights, but they didn't like to go too early. On their new wages there was not much for drink.

Keir was sitting in his favourite corner, finishing his homework. Once he had left it to the last minute, but now he liked to finish it on Friday so that the rest of the weekend was free for the pictures or the chapel social, and the Sunday evening service and the walk in the dark that followed it. At chapel he had made friends with a boy who was a year older than he was, and in the first year of the Sixth; and the pair of them had met two girls from the Girls' Grammar School, two sisters called Gwen and Lila Peterson. They never met during the week. The Girls' Grammar School was on the far side of the city and outside the three-mile-limit, so the girls had passes. Keir still walked to school, but he had given up going with Chas, and walked with David, with that funny little lad Jimmy Metcalf still tagging on behind them.

It was Gwen and Lila that they went walking with every Sunday night after chapel. The four of them never made an appointment, but they always seemed to meet at the same place and the same time. Sometimes, if there was no social, they would sit together in the back seat of the cinema. During the walk they used to separate and Keir went with Gwen, the younger of the sisters. She had beautiful brown eyes and very soft hands, and she used a scent called Californian Poppy.

Mr and Mrs Peterson were very friendly and hospitable and often invited David and Keir to their house in Windsor Gardens, not far away from Mr Futers. A year ago, wild horses would not have got Keir to Windsor Gardens, but now he loved to go there. Mr Peterson worked in Durham as a County Council clerk in the Shire Hall, but his great passion was the stage. From time-to-time he organised concerts in the chapel schoolroom, and it was then that he came into his own. Keir's father said that Herbert had once been on the stage, and whether it was true or not he was a born entertainer. David's father was a serious and humourless man, and their house was a cold and cheerless place with dark photographs of famous Methodist preachers in black frames on the walls, and a family bible in the middle of the square bare mahogany table. But no bible ever stood on Herbert Peterson's table, and no gloomy photographs darkened his walls. Instead of Mr Harland's organ with its hymn book there was a piano with shining brass candle-sconces; instead of his cold mahogany table and horsehair chairs there were soft easy chairs, a trolley on which the sandwiches were wheeled in, and bright curtains that you pulled open and closed by means of tasselled cords. This was Herbert's rehearsal and concert room. Here his two daughters hammered away at their duets. Here he sang to his wife's accompaniment, 'Grandfather's Clock', 'When Father papered the parlour', and 'The Old Rugged Cross'. Here he would dress up to do his famous turns, for he was a good mimic and he could take off Charlie Chaplin and Harry Lauder. Here he would bang away himself at 'Clementine', 'Camptown Races', and 'Jerusalem', and jolly everyone into joining in the choruses.

Keir envied this family. They could all play the piano and Herbert could get a tune even out of a penny whistle. Keir was a duffer at music, and a musical score was a foreign language to him. His voice was breaking and when he tried to join in the singing he would find his voice shooting up into a comical squeak on one note and subsiding into a gruff bass at the next. Herbert laughed till he had to wipe the tears from his eyes, and Gwen and Lila were nearly as bad. Keir blushed and wriggled, but he did not feel too much of a fool.

These evenings were only the rehearsals for the great public performances, the concerts in the schoolroom, where Herbert came into his own. He warmed the audience up with a few jokes, led his concert party through 'The Lost Chord' and 'All Through the Night', introduced Harry Gill who sang 'The Miller of Dee' and then 'In a Monastery Garden', disappeared behind a screen while Harry was taking the limelight, to reappear as Harry Lauder with kilt and twisted stick to sing 'Roaming in the Gloaming' and 'A Wee House in the Corrie', vanished again while Gwen and Lila thumped through their duets, and came back to finish off the concert leading his choir in 'The Bells of Aberdovey'.

Keir enjoyed the concerts, but he enjoyed them most when Gwen sang. It hardly mattered what she sang. He liked to look at her and to listen to her.

The Petersons and the Harlands were the kind of people he had never met before. They were a cut above him. Their houses were so much posher. He often wondered what Gwen would think if he invited her to Brunel Street with its cold sitting-room and its outside ash closet. And these new friends of his seemed to have so much to look forward to. Gwen and Lila were preparing to go to a Teachers' Training College. David was going to medical school in Edinburgh. He was to be a dentist. Even Chas had his future mapped out for him in the Civil Service, whatever that was. But Keir didn't know what he was heading for. His father and mother had never spoken to him of these things.

He looked up from his work to listen to his father. His marra had come and they were both sitting in front of the fire, talking as they often did, about their work and about the future. The failure of the strike had brought great bitterness to Keir's father, and for the first time in his life his spirit had begun to fail him.

'I'll tell tha my opinion, Billy,' he was saying. 'This country has chucked away the best servants they ivver had. Things will nivver be the same, nivver. 'Cos the miners will nivver forget the way they've been treated the last few months. But there'll be a day of reckoning, Billy—mebbe not in our time, but, as sure as God's my judge, it'll come. And one of these days the country will hev to pay for what they've done to us. They've made us bloody-minded, Billy. Humiliated—that's what we've been. But ye canna dee this to men and women and get away wi' it for ivver. Ye winna see this in Old Moore's Almanac, but I tell tha, Billy, the strike was a failure—but it wasn't the finish. No, lad, it was just the start.'

'Aye, I think tha's reet, Davy.'

They sat silent for a few moments and Mr Ramsay turned to look at his son. During the long months of the strike father and son had drifted apart. Just when he had the time and the opportunity to draw nearer to his son, anxiety and bitterness had driven him further away from his boy. But the affair of the cundy had made him realise that Keir was no longer the boy whose stupid pranks and thoughtless ways had brought him almost to the brink of expulsion. He was growing up. A fringe of hair was beginning to darken his upper lip. He was learning to work with intensity and concentration.

All the father's hopes and plans for a better future for himself and his fellow-workers were in ruins. All the sacrifices and hardships of the last few months had brought them nothing but humiliation. They were the defeated ones, compelled, for all their courage, to submit in the end, to knuckle under and accept the shameful terms they had so indignantly rejected. But his son did not look defeated. As his hand travelled swiftly and confidently over the pages of his exercise books he seemed to be inscribing some new kind of destiny for himself.

The old man remembered how Percy Metcalf had repeated something to him that he had already said to Keir.

'Give that lad some encouragement, Davy. Ye nivver knaa. Ye might hev a future Labour member of Parliament there.'

Maybe after all the fight was not wholly lost. Maybe it would be taken up again, to be fought in a new arena and by a new generation.

Davy Ramsay, once more hewer at the coal face at the Bishop Pit, felt sore. His muscles were aching—it was very difficult for a middle-aged man to go back to the coal face after months of idleness—and his heart was saddened by the consciousness of failure. But there was no sense of defeat on the face of his son. All he could see there was a new confidence, a pride in mastering a new world.

SEVEN

The Exam

Mr Howard, who was in charge of the School Certificate exam, took up the paper knife from his desk and with one quick movement slit open the brown envelope.

'You must on no account turn over this paper till I tell you,' he said, then went rapidly up and down the rows of desks leaving the question papers face down. Then, when he had finished, he looked at his watch, waited a few seconds and then said, 'Right! Turn over the paper and begin—now!'

Keir turned over the paper. It was the first printed question paper he had ever seen, the first he had ever been called upon to do. He ran quickly through the questions. They were not too difficult. They were what he had expected. He looked round and saw Chas—his face white—biting his lips. Then Keir dipped his pen in the inkwell, and began.

For the next two hours—for the rest of his life—his father and mother, the streets, the adventure of the cundy, the night when he had seen the Bishop holding up his cross, the sad evening when his father learnt that the long fight with the coal owners had been lost—all receded from him and sank out of his mind. There were new things he had to face, and he knew they had no terrors for him. Revelling in his new-found command, he wrote on, clearly and firmly and happily.